JEFF RISELEY

FOUNDER OF THE SALES HEALTH ALLIANCE

STRESS LESS, SELL MORE

220 WAYS TO

Prioritize Your Well-Being, Prevent Burnout, and Hit Your Sales Target

WILEY

Published by John Wiley & Sons, Inc., Hoboken, New Jersey.
Published simultaneously in Canada.

For general information on our other products and services or for technical support, please contact our Customer Care Department within the United States at (800) 762-2974, outside the United States at (317) 572-3993 or fax (317) 572-4002.

Wiley also publishes its books in a variety of electronic formats. Some content that appears in print may not be available in electronic formats. For more information about Wiley products, visit our web site at www.wiley.com.

Library of Congress Cataloging-in-Publication Data

Names: Riseley, Jeff, author.
Title: Stress less, sell more : 220 ways to prioritize your well-being,
   prevent burnout, and hit your sales target / Jeff Riseley.
Description: Hoboken, New Jersey : John Wiley & Sons, Inc., [2023] |
   Includes bibliographical references and index.
Identifiers: LCCN 2022047801 (print) | LCCN 2022047802 (ebook) | ISBN
   9781394153398 (cloth) | ISBN 9781394153411 (adobe pdf) | ISBN
   9781394153404 (epub)
Subjects: LCSH: Stress (Psychology) | Well-being. | Selling. | Stress
   management. | Success in business.
Classification: LCC BF575.S75 R57 2023 (print) | LCC BF575.S75 (ebook) |
   DDC 155.9/042—dc23/eng/20221116
LC record available at https://lccn.loc.gov/2022047801
LC ebook record available at https://lccn.loc.gov/2022047802

Cover Design: Wiley
Cover Image: © bubaone/DigitalVision Vectors/Getty Images

SKY10039813_120922

Dedicated to Taylor, my parents, and my close group of friends who continue to support and challenge me to grow every single day.

Contents

How to Use This Book

WORKING IN SALES can be extremely stressful, and most salespeople I've worked with over the years have agreed with this statement: **When salespeople stress less, they sell more.**

When sales teams and sales reps become anxious, depressed, or experience burnout, their sales performance and mental health suffers. If you factor in weekends, holidays, vacations, wellness days, sick days, and unforeseen events that take you away from your sales role, there are roughly 220 "selling" days a year.

This book was created to help you better navigate the pressure and stressors you face during those 220 days in a mentally healthy way. Each page or two will tackle a different aspect of *mental health in sales*. Some will be informative and draw on learnings from the latest workplace research, some may simply challenge you to think about mental health in a different way, while other pages will be more tactical and equip you with mindset, resilience, and stress-management strategies you can start using right away.

You, as the reader, have the choice to read it day by day or all at once. If you're part of a sales team, I'd recommend going through this book together. Try reading each page separately and then discussing as a group during your daily sales stand-ups.

In addition to the information contained in these pages, Sales Health Alliance was created to be a resource first and business second. This means the links found in this book will direct you back to the 100 free articles and videos living on the website, in addition to some paid services we offer.

Change happens when small, consistent actions are taken daily to form habits. My hope is this book leads to the creation of some good habits that help you maximize your sales performance and mental health each day.

Jeff Riseley
Founder
Sales Health Alliance

JANUARY

JANUARY, Day 01: Quota Relief

I recently learned that companies like HubSpot offer their salespeople quota relief when they take vacations. Can we just agree that this should 100% be the norm for all salespeople everywhere?

At their core, quotas and sales targets should be nothing more than a challenging yet achievable goal that helps provide an individual sales rep with direction in their role. We encounter problems with them when the intention behind them changes, and they are viewed by leadership as a tool to control human behavior and impose obedience. Sadly, the latter is often the case and can be seen with vacation policies.

Any company touting "unlimited PTO" without offering quota relief is operating from a belief (whether they know it or not) that quota will keep salespeople obedient and "keep the policy in check." Salespeople aren't naïve—we know this. Actions speak louder than words, and offering your salespeople quota relief when they take vacations is one of the best ways to show your team that you *trust* them to be responsible adults.

In addition to building more trusting relationships, teams can also expect a boost in mental health and sales performance. As Kevin Bailey from Dreamfuel taught me, feeling *guilty* is a very powerful emotion that makes it incredibly difficult to recover from stress and use our time off to effectively recharge. That's why I believe we can remove this feeling of guilt by offering quota relief so our salespeople can *actually* come back feeling their best and perform their best.

JANUARY, Day 02: Compounding Health

LeBron James spends an estimated $1.5 million a year on his mind and body. That's about 4% of his salary this year. How would you spend 4% of your salary to do the same?

LeBron has been the greatest for the *longest* with no signs of slowing down at age 36. A lot of this has to do with how well he treats his body—something salespeople are notoriously bad at during stressful months.

Here are some investments and routines I've made to help improve my physical and mental health to ensure I'm showing up in my peak state every day.

- **New mattress and pillows:** For better sleep.
- **Standing desk:** For better energy.
- **Ergonomic desk chair:** For better posture.
- **WHOOP tracker:** For better training and recovery.
- **Brita filter:** For better water.
- **Dyson air purifier:** For better air.
- **Peloton bike:** For better cardio.
- **Bodylastics:** For better strength.
- **Regular chiropractic treatments:** For better stress management.
- **Cold showers:** For a better immune system.
- **Read at least 10 pages per day:** For better knowledge.
- **Daily gratitude and meditation:** For a better mindset.
- **Meal plan:** For daily salads, nutrients, and vitamins.

If you improve the inputs going into your body by just 1%, these inputs are going to compound over time into a much happier, healthier, and successful sales career.

JANUARY, Day 03: PIP 2.0

The PIP, aka the "Performance Improvement Plan," has to be one of the dumbest things the sales industry has ever created, and this is why:

Humans have a highly evolved "social protection system," which helped our ancestors survive and reproduce effectively by being part of a tribe. When we feel pushed to the edge of our "tribe," like when we're handed a PIP, we perceive this as *danger* and an extremely vulnerable position to be in. Fear kicks our body into fight-or-flight, and the overflow of stress hormones that get released shuts down our ability to sell effectively.

To make things worse, there is a lot we *cannot* control within sales that can affect the outcome. It's like a coach saying to a basketball player: *"I don't care what happens—go score 25 points in the game tomorrow or you're going to be traded to a new team."*

What should we do instead?

Enter PIP 2.0—the "PRACTICE Improvement Plan"

The best athletes and salespeople know that when their performance has declined, the best thing they can do is practice. They can get more shots up, they can make more calls, they can practice their pitch, and they ask new questions.

Ultimately, they can invest more *effort* into the things they *can* control that will lead to better performance outcomes over time. Framing this effort as practice also helps keep the focus on learning and growth as the motivator rather than fear and threatening outcomes or consequences.

JANUARY, Day 04: Sales Sabbaticals

Sales sabbaticals were extremely common for salespeople who could afford them during and after COVID. Top salespeople who had disposable income quit companies and left high-paying roles to put their career on hold. Many sales organizations were caught off guard by this trend and still don't understand why sabbaticals became popular, so here is what happened.

During COVID, salespeople were working under extremely high levels of stress without having access to popular stress management activities such as exercise, social events, or travel to help release the buildup of tension. As a result, employees were heavily relying on *willpower* to force themselves to push through their work tasks, without the ability to rest and recover effectively.

Willpower works a lot like an elastic band, and the more we rely on it, the more tension builds up until it breaks or is released. When this happens it snaps back *past* the point where it started and creates an overcorrection (The Great Resignation). This is why if a dieter who is attempting to make big changes to eating habits using willpower doesn't cheat a little, they cheat *a lot* when willpower finally runs out.

One- and two-week vacations were no longer enough to cope with the pressure of life during the pandemic. The Great Resignation occurred, and companies were left scrambling as top performers walked out and didn't come back. Unfortunately, this pattern of sabbaticals and extended time off is likely to continue in a cyclical pattern because life-changing stressors created by events associated with political turmoil, recessions, climate change, and overpopulation are only going to become more frequent in the future. Collectively we have to move away from our overreliance on willpower at work, and sales organizations need to realize their salespeople need additional support in coping with these external stressors.

JANUARY, Day 05: Intrinsic Motivation

I have met very few salespeople who would describe themselves as intrinsically motivated by the work they do in sales. This has led me to ask the question, *Is working in sales actually that boring, or is something else going on?*

To answer this question we need to understand the difference between intrinsic and extrinsic motivation. Salespeople who are extrinsically motivated sell because of what they will get, such as the promotions, commission checks, and vacations. Salespeople who are intrinsically motivated sell because they simply enjoy selling, which they perceive as interesting and meaningful for its own sake.

Boatloads of research from Alfie Kohn in his book *Punished by Rewards*,[1] has shown that the QUALITY of performance, *creativity*, and *learning* tends to decline significantly when people are extrinsically motivated, which means sales leaders should be striving to have teams that are intrinsically motivated.

This is challenging because the average sales environment is set up to kill intrinsic motivation. Research has shown that intrinsic motivation declines in people when they feel:

- Threatened;
- Watched;
- Forced to work under a deadline;
- Ordered around;
- Made to compete against other people.

Sound familiar to working in sales?

Decades of creating the wrong sales environments has conditioned an entire industry focused on "performance" to actually underperform. Time to break the pattern and build an environment where people thrive.

JANUARY, Day 06: Work Hard, Play Hard

If you're interviewing for a sales role, and they describe their company culture as "Work hard, play hard," be careful. In my experience this simple statement usually means you'll be working in an environment with the following:

- Profits over people;
- Machine-like metrics;
- Selfishness;
- Company politics;
- No boundaries;
- No rest and recovery;
- Carrot holding and chasing;
- Weak leadership;
- Weak mentorship;
- Low personal development;
- Low trust;
- Heavy party culture;
- High burnout and attrition rate;
- Mental health stigma.

There is also usually the potential to make big $$$ in organizations like this, but is it worth it? It's easy to get stuck wearing "golden handcuffs" and feel trapped in an environment that stunts your growth because it can be hard to replace the large salary and high commission somewhere else. My two recommendations for situations like this are:

1. **If you take the job, then have a plan.**

   Get in, make your money, and get out. Mitigate your lifestyle to avoid expensive habits so you feel less trapped. Last thing you want to do is find yourself in a situation where you're working in a toxic environment but can't leave because you're paying off a Mercedes you shouldn't have purchased in the first place.

2. Look for companies that describe their sales culture differently:

"People achieve their goals inside and outside of work."
"Work hard, recover hard."
"Practice openness, candor, and vulnerability."
"Embrace and learn from failure."

Before going for your next job interview ask yourself this question and answer it honestly so you know what to look for: How would you want a future employer to describe their culture that would match your needs and core values?

JANUARY, Day 07: Kobe

In an interview with Lewis Howes, Kobe Bryant shared a story about a time when he was 10 years old and played basketball for an entire summer.[2] During this summer he didn't score a single point. When he was crying about it, his dad came over to him and gave him a hug and said, "I don't care if you score zero points or you score 60 points; I'm going to love you no matter what." Kobe said that gave him all of the confidence in the world to fail.

From there he went to work and adopted a **long-term view.** He wasn't going to catch the kids ahead of him in a day, in a week, or even in a year. He put more thought and effort into learning and practicing the fundamentals of his craft. Over time he caught those who relied primarily on their athletic gifts and evolved into a legend through effort and practice.

This is what happens when we put less emphasis on outcomes and give people a safe environment to learn from failure. We allow them to fall in love with the process and enjoy developing their craft even in the face of adversity.

Over time they become legends.

Are you a sales leader with enough courage and trust to tell a new rep today, "I don't care if you make zero sales this month or you make 20 sales this month; I'm going to support you no matter what"? Who knows, you might have a mini Kobe Bryant on your team who just needs a little support and a different environment for them to flourish into a superstar.

JANUARY, Day 08: The Problem with Slack

Unpopular question: Is it time to delete Slack?

Much like Facebook, I think it started with the right intentions, but most teams are no longer using it for the right reasons. Lately I've heard it being described as an "interruption tool" and "gossip tool" while operating under the guise of a way to boost productivity and team collaboration.

Here Are Some Numbers for You:

1. Gloria Mark, a professor at the University of California, Irvine, found workers only spend 10 and a half minutes on a task before being interrupted.[3] When the average worker is interrupted it takes them about 23 minutes to return to the original task, and this delay in completing tasks increases stress and burnout. Even more shocking, 56% of interruptions are from external sources and 44% are created by ourselves.
2. According to the American Psychological Association, shifting between tasks can cost as much as 40% of someone's productivity time.[4] Not to mention the "Slack culture" that demands immediate responses and actively erodes boundaries between work and home with the inability to disconnect.

As more and more new hires onboard remotely, I see too many organizations defaulting to relationship building through Slack, because it's easier than having a phone call. This makes interruptions feel unrelenting and makes it difficult for new hires to integrate into a team's culture quickly.

Today, combat this and if someone is new to your team, schedule time to get to know them outside of Slack. Improving relationships offline will always lead to better communication online.

JANUARY, Day 09: Slack Hygiene

When I asked my network if it's time to delete Slack, several people commented on the LinkedIn post. Here is a summary of the main learnings from everyone that shared their thoughts on the topic:

1. Slack is extremely helpful when used the right way.
2. Misuse negatively affects deep work, deep focus, and mental health.
3. Individuals need to build strong boundaries and use self-control.
4. Use the "snooze" and "away" buttons frequently.
5. The phone app is totally unnecessary while working from home.
6. Leadership should not assume people use Slack in a healthy way. Run Slack "hygiene" and communication training.
7. Leadership needs to set clear expectations with the team from day 1.
8. Leadership needs to stop using it to micromanage and check who is "on."
9. Remote onboarding is creating bad habits without training.
10. Use it to replace short phone calls, not important meetings.
11. Bullying, abuse, and shaming happens on Slack. Don't "like" these comments.
12. It's easy for new hires to misperceive and be offended by comments without a prior working relationship.
13. If something is urgent, *use* the phone; expect delays with Slack.

What would you add to the list of Slack best practices and practice with your team?

JANUARY, Day 10: Eight Rules to Live By

Recently, it was my four-year anniversary of being cancer free. This sparked a lot of self-reflection of what has happened in my life since the diagnosis. I've put together my eight rules for life inside and outside of sales that I've learned over the past few years.

#1 – Seek Discomfort

Accelerated growth and the most meaningful life experiences happen outside our comfort zone. When we seek discomfort on a regular basis, we can rewire our anxiety from a "threat" detector to a "growth" detector. This is an important skill to develop because both sales and life in general can feel uncomfortable at times. Over time, learning to seek discomfort gets easier and leads to greater levels of personal growth and fulfillment. Having a helpful set of stress management tools and self-care strategies can help you push through the self-doubt, fear, and anxiety you face on the edge of your comfort zone.

#2 – Try to Inspire Instead of Impress

Too many of us spend every waking hour trying to impress our friends, partners, colleagues, bosses, and buyers. This traps us into thinking who we "should be" versus who we actually are. Instead, focus on inspiring others through your quirks, journey, authenticity, generosity, empathy, compassion, discipline, and hard work. These qualities and actions are firmly in your hands to control every single day.

#3 – The 8-Hour Workday Makes No Sense

Any company or leader that is operating under the expectation that a human being can focus and complete high-quality work for seven to eight hours (or more) per day is living in a fantasy. According to research and productivity experts, on the best days, we'll have four, maybe five hours of deep focus time.[5] This means companies and leaders need to stop focusing and rewarding those on their team who are working the longest. Instead their focus should be on removing distractions and maximizing recovery periods to generate the highest performance possible during these four to five hours each day.

You can continue reading rules #4 through #8 by scanning here and sharing the full list with someone on your team who could benefit from them.

JANUARY, Day 11: Take Your Breaks

Feeling that Zoom fatigue today? Microsoft did some research recently to prove that your brain needs breaks.[6]

The researchers conducted brain scans on 14 people during four half-hour back-to-back meetings, one without breaks and one with 10-minute breaks in-between each meeting. What they uncovered was that those working without breaks experienced higher stress levels; in particular, stress levels spiked while participants transitioned between meetings when there was no break and experienced lower levels of engagement in the next meeting. Long story short, performance suffered when recovery periods were neglected.

Between demos with clients and internal meetings, it's *very* easy for a salesperson to have a calendar that is filled with back-to-back calls. If you want to perform your best, then you need to protect your calendar and schedule breaks. Learn to tell your manager *and* clients:

"No—that time doesn't work. Can we move it back by 10 minutes?"

To the sales leaders reading this book, try shortening your meetings to 20 or 40 minutes to ensure your team has time to reset before their next meeting. This will make everyone more productive and help keep stress levels under control throughout the day.

JANUARY, Day 12: The Problem with Process

Did you know the keyboard we're all typing on right now was intentionally designed to be inefficient? That's right. The QWERTY keyboard had two primary purposes when it was first designed:

1. It was designed to slow down typing speed, because if you typed too fast on the original typewriter it would jam.
2. It was designed so salespeople could quickly type the word "Typewriter" only using the top line of keys to demonstrate how efficient it was.

Ozan Varol cleverly uses this example in his book *Think Like a Rocket Scientist* to highlight how "process" is by definition backward looking and developed in response to yesterday's troubles.[7] If we don't challenge it, we'll never progress.

Enter the five-day work week—created during the industrial revolution in 1908, when work was primarily blue collar. This "process" is dated, inefficient, and taking a toll on mental health. Our work has now become increasingly remote, white collar, and computers/technology have us working at breakneck speeds that have drastically reduced our ability to rest and recover.

Research is piling up that we're getting this work process wrong. For example, when Microsoft Japan experimented with a four-day work week, productivity rose by nearly 40%.[8]

Today, start thinking about what "processes" you're still following that are no longer relevant and affecting your overall mental health. A good way to do this is to evaluate your daily habits or routines that have been on autopilot for a few years and update them for present-day you. How can you create a work week or make changes that help you thrive today, instead of yesterday?

JANUARY, Day 13: VP Sales Enablement

I'm curious to see which company is going to be first to hire a VP Sales Enablement of Well-Being. For those interested, here is a job description to help you get started:

The VP Sales Enablement of Well-Being position was created to help optimize sales team performance at X company through better mental health and well-being. Your main mission is to ensure each member of our sales team is showing up well rested, managing stress effectively, and feeling their best so they can optimally perform for our customers.

Key responsibilities include:

- Design, lead, and provide training that improves sales team resilience, EQ, and mental health.
- Be a confidant for frontline managers and individual contributors.
- Implement well-being KPIs to manage burnout.
- Relay sales team well-being reporting and analysis to upper management.
- Work with CRO to set balanced sales targets.
- Develop processes that promote "active recovery" of the sales team.
- Build mental health and resilience processes into new hire onboarding.
- Work with HR to evaluate and provide mental health service providers.
- Design processes to improve openness, inclusivity, and vulnerability within sales.

How would you finish this job description and what type of qualifications do you think this person should have?

If you're curious to learn more about what the Sales Enablement of Well-Being is and how it applies to sales, scan here to read why it will help sales teams exponentially improve performance.

JANUARY, Day 14: Interview Questions

If you're a salesperson looking for a job who wants to avoid a toxic environment and find one that supports better mental health, I've created a list of questions you can ask during the interview process:

- What did you do to support your team's mental health during COVID?
- What type of mental health training or services has the company invested into?
- How important do you think mental health and team well-being is to sales performance?
- How would you react if a sales rep requested a mental health day and they were behind target?
- At the end of a challenging month, how do you encourage teams to rest and recover?
- Even the best salespeople miss target sometimes; how is a sales rep treated when they miss their target?

If asking these questions makes you uncomfortable, then that's a good sign. You're stepping outside your comfort zone and learning to put your needs first. If asking these questions disqualifies you from the interview process, then you can feel good about that too. You saved yourself from a bad situation. If asking these questions are met with a blank stare, hums and haws, or an attempt to deflect the question . . .

Run.

Finally, if you're a sales leader or hiring manager reading this right now and not proud of how you would answer these questions, then it's time to change.

Check out some bonus questions in this article and share them with a fellow salesperson who is currently in the interview process, by scanning here.

JANUARY, Day 15: LeBron James

If sales leaders coached LeBron James like most manage their salespeople, their interaction might look something like this:

Sales leader:	*"We're on a six-game winning streak* (consecutive quarters hit); *we need to keep crushing our opponents."*
LeBron:	*"Sure, coach."*
Sales leader:	*"LeBron, instead of getting 30 points and 10 rebounds like the last game, I need you to get 40 points and 15 rebounds this game."* (Metrics)
LeBron:	*"Why, coach?"*
Sales leader:	*"We need more fans. Our sold-out stadiums aren't enough to make us happy."* (Rat Race)
LeBron:	*"Coach . . . I can try, but I'm feeling a little burnt out from that road trip and back-to-back games."* (Hard previous quarters)
Sales leader:	*"Burnt out? Really? Here are some new basketball shoes—they'll make you run faster* (sales technology). *And let me teach you a better way to shoot so it's easier to score."* (Sales training)
LeBron:	*"Coach . . . I think I just need some rest. Maybe manage my minutes* (lower my metrics) *in the next game so I can rest and not get hurt?"*
Sales leader:	*"No, we need to win this game."* (Hit sales target) *"Didn't you hear me? We need to crush it, or the world will end."*

LeBron plays the next game, tears his ACL, and changes teams in free agency.

Sales leader:	*"Man, LeBron was a bad culture fit and not cut out for basketball."*

JANUARY, Day 16: Daily Vitamins

Most people treat self-care like an aspirin when they should be treating it like a daily multivitamin. In order for self-care to be effective in supporting our mental health, it requires consistent daily practice.

Think about it, when we have a headache, we take some aspirin and within a few hours we start to feel better. Whereas, in order for vitamins to be effective in keeping us healthy and ward off diseases we have to take them daily. We encounter problems when we try to apply this "aspirin" self-care strategy to our mental health and well-being:

We go to the gym when we feel out of shape, work out for a week until we feel a little better, and then *stop*. We try meditating when we're overwhelmed, it works a bit, enough to feel better, and then *stop*.

Self-Care Is Like a Multivitamin for Your Brain

It helps build resilience and protect our mental health, but only if it's practiced and used daily. The best way to do this is to bookend your workday with a start-up and wind-down routine that includes self-care.

This is my process:

Start-up routine:

- Personal development reading;
- Workout;
- Cold shower;
- Wim Hof breathing method;
- Visualization.

Wind-down routine:

- Reflect on progress made;
- Make a plan for the next day;
- Gratitude;
- Journal;
- Meditation.

By bookending your day with a self-care routine, you make sure you take your brain vitamins daily, and the routine trains your body to easily move from work mode to relax mode. This is especially important to do while working from home.

If you try to change too many things about your routine and habits all at once, it won't be sustainable. Start by adding one additional self-care routine to the beginning or end of every day. Complete it every day for a week, and see how you feel. Then plan to add another one.

JANUARY, Day 17: Advice from a Friend

If you're trapped in a downward spiral and feeling stressed, anxious, or burned-out today, try asking yourself this one simple question:

"If my best friend was feeling the way I am right now, What would I tell them to do?"

You might tell them to:

- Go for a walk;
- Don't skip lunch and eat something;
- Spend time with friends or family;
- Leave work on time and have a self-care night;
- Go for a massage;
- Make a plan;
- Tell your boss how you feel;
- Make a pros and cons list;
- Get a good night's sleep;
- Take a mental health day;
- Delegate some work to a colleague;
- Plan a vacation;
- Journal;
- Meditate;
- Go to the gym.

Whether we're an expert on mental health or not, we all know how to give good advice and help friends when they are in need. When we're trapped in a downward spiral, we lose focus and often think working more is the only way to make ourselves feel better. This makes everything worse. We forget about all these awesome ideas because we've lost perspective and our brains are stuck processing our own emotions.

Break the cycle, and ask yourself that question today because it will help you find your way out.

JANUARY, Day 18: Remove Your Blockers

When we're feeling overwhelmed, burned out, or stressed, sometimes it can feel as if our only option is to take a break, vacation, or quit. But there is a second option, which involves identifying and removing our *blockers*.

Far too often we find ourselves operating on autopilot, using the same routine, and following the same process day in and day out. This can be applicable to how we approach sales, dating, conversations with others, fitness, and our own mental health. As we grow and develop or we change environments, sometimes our routines and processes are no longer relevant to our new situation. But we keep following them because we've become addicted to them.

Like trying to squeeze a square peg into a circular hole, we add extra frustration and friction to our lives that builds up over time. Rather than optimize our trusted processes and routines for a new you and a new environment, we keep using them because they have provided safety, stability, and confidence in our lives for years. Instead of looking inwards, we look outwards and look to blame the internal buildup of frustration on other people, companies, economies, weather, and politics, things we ultimately have very little control over.

That's why it's important to remember that we *always* have full control of our process and our routines. Sometimes we just need to update them and remove the blockers in our process that are holding us back from who we are now and where we're trying to go. So what's something in your control that is blocking you today?

JANUARY, Day 19: Hiring Process Burnout

We need to acknowledge that most sales hiring processes are burning people out *before* they even start working for a company.

Think about it, the hiring process for a typical sales role at most companies usually involves roughly three rounds of interviews followed by a project or case study presentation. This is a *big* ask for someone already working full time and carrying a quota elsewhere. Then multiply the pressure of this single hiring process by three or five given most job seekers are going through the same process simultaneously with multiple companies. Also, factor in that most candidates are likely working in an environment they don't like, hence why they're looking for a job, which means stress, anxiety, and pressure are already *very* high.

Then the cherry on top—sales leaders and hiring managers love to end their hiring process by asking their future hire a very stupid question:

"So when is the earliest you can start?"

Obviously most job seekers will say "ASAP" out of fear of losing the opportunity they just secured. Two weeks later the rep, leader, and hiring manager are all wondering why learning and performance is below average. This underperformance is caused by hiring process burnout and the grueling effort of hunting for a job in the twenty-first century, while simultaneously working north of 40 hours a week elsewhere.

Sales reps, don't be afraid to ask for an adequate amount of time off before starting a new job so you can decompress and hit the ground running. Leaders, if you want to stop hiring people who are burned out, then stop asking the question above.

Instead end your hiring process by saying:

"We understand looking for a job is stressful. How much time do you need to recover and get your mind right so you can hit the ground running? What do you need from our end to support you?"

JANUARY, Day 20: Sharing Bad Habits

What do you do when you start to become anxious or depressed?
Maybe you:

- Stay in bed longer than normal;
- Drink more alcohol than normal;
- Become more irritable than normal;
- Scroll on social media more than normal;
- Exercise less than normal;
- Go outside less than normal;
- Play more video games than normal;
- Be less sociable than normal;
- Smile less than normal;
- Talk less than normal;
- Exert less effort than normal;
- Cook less than normal;
- Set higher expectations than normal.

These are all examples of micro-changes in behavior that may happen when our mental health starts to decline. The problem is most of the time we're unaware of when we start doing them. This means it's important to have a mental health buddy system with a friend, partner, and/or colleague. Share your main behavioral changes with them so they know what to look out for. Let them know it's okay to check in on you and say, "Hey, if you see me doing X, Y, Z, do you mind checking in on me?"

Sales leaders, this is absolutely critical for you too. It's okay to not be okay. You don't have to have all the answers all the time. Give your team members permission to check in on you as well. This will inject a healthy dose of vulnerability and trust into your team.

JANUARY Endnotes

1. Kohn, A. (1999). *Punished by Rewards: The trouble with gold stars, incentive plans, A's, praise and other bribes.* Houghton Mifflin (Trade).
2. Howes, L. "Kobe Bryant's Last Great Interview on The Mindset of a Winner & How to Succeed." Lewis Howes. September 10, 2018. https://youtu.be/WY0wONSarXA.
3. Mark, G., Czerwinski, M., and Iqbal, S. T. (2018). "Effects of individual differences in blocking workplace distractions." Proceedings of the 2018 CHI Conference on Human Factors in Computing Systems.

4. "Multitasking: Switching Costs." American Psychological Association, March 20, 2006. https://www.apa.org/topics/research/multitasking.
5. Wiginton, K. "Your Ability to Focus May Be Limited to 4 or 5 Hours a Day. Here's How to Make the Most of Them." *Washington Post*, June 1, 2021. https://www.washingtonpost.com/lifestyle/wellness/productivity-focus-work-tips/2021/05/31/07453934-bfd0-11eb-b26e-53663e6be6ff_story.html.
6. "Research Proves Your Brain Needs Breaks." Microsoft, April 20, 2021. https://www.microsoft.com/en-us/worklab/work-trend-index/brain-research.
7. Varol, O. (2021). *Think Like a Rocket Scientist: Simple strategies for giant leaps in work and life*. W H Allen.
8. Chappell, B. "4-Day Workweek Boosted Workers' Productivity by 40%, Microsoft Japan Says." NPR, November 4, 2019. https://www.npr.org/2019/11/04/776163853/microsoft-japan-says-4-day-workweek-boosted-workers-productivity-by-40.

FEBRUARY

FEBRUARY, Day 21: Listen to Your Body

In 2021, I took a mental health day with four working days left, before my week-long vacation. There is a lot of stigma around doing this, but here is why I did it.

In the weeks leading up to my vacation, I was pushing myself extremely hard to finish several client projects I had been juggling. As a result of overstretching myself, I'd started feeling more irritable than usual, experiencing very restless sleep and thinking about work 24/7, all signs of burnout.

In addition to feeling burnt out, my week-long vacation would involve my first flight in three years (COVID and starting a business made traveling difficult) to a place I had never visited before. We often forget that flying, time zone changes, and a new environment can add tremendous stress to the body, even when they are in the context of a vacation.

So I had a decision to make, keep pushing, run my body further into the ground, enter my vacation on "empty," and run the risk of getting sick, or take a mental health day, reset my mind and body so I could finish the final few working days strong, and enter my vacation with some gas in the tank to maximize my recovery. I chose the latter.

In our society, far too many of us are just "trying to make it" to our vacations, which means we enter our vacations totally burnt out, which in turn prevents us from recharging effectively. Burnout doesn't care about your deadlines, projects, or timelines, and it's your body's way to slow you down, when you won't slow down yourself. If you need a mini unplug or mental health day right before your vacation, take it. It will pay off in your performance long term when you can maximize enjoyment of your vacation and come back more rested and recharged.

FEBRUARY, Day 22: Stop the Hamster Wheels

Sales organizations that are having trouble retaining top sales talent beyond the two- to three-year mark can benefit from building a one-to two-month sales sabbatical into their employee experience for tenured salespeople.

Between the daily metrics and sales targets it doesn't take long for a salesperson to start feeling stuck running on a hamster wheel. Round and round every month or quarter. In my experience, this feeling really starts to set in around the two-and-a-half-year mark once the early career milestones wear off (for example, account executive to senior account executive) and future career progression within a company feels limited. Compound this with two-and-a-half years of mounting stress and burnout, and it becomes very easy for reps to start asking themselves, "What's the point of all this?" So most quit, get off the hamster wheel, and try to find meaning elsewhere, only to find themselves repeating the process two years later.

Sales organizations can combat this cycle by helping reps find more purpose in their work. This can be achieved through a sales sabbatical that allows top salespeople to travel, explore, and regain perspective on their long-term goals in life.

More importantly, it keeps leaders and the organizations accountable. So they stop building hamster wheels and instead build places people want to come back to, that align with their long-term goals and purpose.

FEBRUARY, Day 23: Being Present

I would argue that the rush we feel when we close a big deal is not primarily due to what we just accomplished but instead a result of finally being able to be present. Every day salespeople are forced to work in an environment where they are constantly perceiving their actions and behaviors through the eyes of others.

- "Will this email make the buyer curious?"
- "What will they think if I call them now?"
- "Is now the right time?"
- "Are they listening to my pitch?"
- "How can I reengage them?"
- "Why might they be ghosting me?"
- "What does my manager think of me?"

This makes it *very* hard to be present. We're always operating on high alert and looking for a threat that may derail a sale and/or seeking approval from others. It's as if we're making thousands of mini social media posts a day that we know will be judged and affect our performance, so we spend hours dissecting them internally. As a result, our anxiety and mental health can spiral out of control.

But when that deal closes, for a brief moment in time, we feel totally safe.

The internal chatter and judgment of our ego can shut off because we're no longer watching ourselves through someone else's eyes. We feel the quiet, peace, calm, and happiness that comes with finally being present.

FEBRUARY, Day 24: Sales Role Models

It's 2022 and many sales cultures are still being influenced by the 90s' pop culture, which glamorized the worst aspects of working in sales. Without proper role models, we'll continue to be stuck in the past. If we want to start building sales cultures that prioritize:

- Customer-centric selling;
- Work-life balance;
- Mental health;
- Inclusivity and diversity;
- Intrinsic motivation;
- Trust and compassion;
- Empathy;
- Psychological safety;
- Vulnerability;

Then we need to stop emulating the salespeople depicted in movies such as *Glengarry Glen Ross*, *Wolf of Wall Street*, *Boiler Room*, *Cadillac Man*, and Gordon Gekko's speeches that encourage and reward:

- Bullying;
- Selfishness;
- Excessive drugs, alcohol, and sex;
- Misogyny;
- Extrinsic motivation;
- Greed;
- Fear;
- Insensitivity;
- Burnout.

Even as I'm writing this, I'm thinking to myself, "How many salespeople are going to read this book and think, 'How uncool is that guy Jeff? Those movies are the best!'" My guess would be maybe 20–30%, which is too much.

Look, I'm not a fan of cancel culture, and those movies are certainly entertaining. Excessive dopamine-driven behaviors, even when watching them on a screen and done by others, are fun to watch but also highly infectious. There is a time and a place for everything, and that time and place for the 90s' pop sales culture was over 20 years ago and in a movie, not as part of our current day-to-day life in sales.

Our sales culture has evolved, expectations have changed, and the line has moved. Visual relics that remind us of crueler and wilder times in sales like the ABC coffee mugs or "Coffee's For Closers" T-shirts are no longer doing us any favors. Now we just need some new forward-thinking pop culture sales icons for the next generation of salespeople to look up to. What would that movie look like to you, and who would you cast?

FEBRUARY, Day 25: Recognition vs Praise

Sales leaders need to start injecting *more* recognition and *less* praise into their weekly sales team meetings. Praising salespeople too much for their achievements and outcomes can create an environment that negatively affects self-esteem over time.

Praise involves comments and feedback from leaders such as:

"Amazing job closing that big deal!"
"I'm impressed by how hard you're working!"
"Great job booking those meetings!"

In situations like this, though well intentioned, praise from sales leaders is being used as a social reward for good behavior and good performance they want to continue. The internal motivator for the salesperson becomes:

"If I do X, I'm rewarded with praise."

This leads to situations where salespeople only feel safe when they are achieving X and receiving praise, so they keep chasing it. Instead, leaders should be focused on providing more recognition, which takes into account the *impact* of who the salesperson is helping.

"Shout out to Jack, whose deal means X, Y, and Z for their client!"
"Shout out to Maggie, whose three meetings helped our team do X, Y, and Z."
"Shout out to Jen, whose new email template is contributing to X, Y, and Z."

It's a subtle, but important difference that combats individualism and keeps the team focused on who they're helping and serving each day.

FEBRUARY, Day 26: Treat Them like Family

Sales leaders, I have a simple ask for you today. If you're about to say or do something to someone on your team today that you wouldn't say or do to your friends, family, or children, then don't do it. This is a simple way to ensure the actions we take as leaders are creating a psychologically safe environment where people can thrive.

Here are a few examples of how you do this if you're a sales manager:

1. Would you give your child an unattainable sales target they had no hope of hitting and then punish them when they came up short?
   Probably not.

2. Would you be condescending to your mom via Slack if she told you she lost a deal she forecasted would close?
   Nope.

3. Would you ask your best friend to work late and message them for updates after hours if you knew they were having trouble sleeping and experiencing burnout?
   Definitely not.

It's very simple science. When people feel safe, they put the team first, are motivated to approach challenges, find creative solutions to problems, and do their best work. When people feel unsafe, they put themselves first, take shortcuts, fear failure, make mistakes, and are more likely to do their worst work.

You have an opportunity to create or destroy safety within your sales team through the micro-actions you take as a leader every single day. Pausing to complete this simple screening process before you act will help you do more creating than destroying on a daily basis.

FEBRUARY, Day 27: Who Will Be More Motivated?

It's important to know the difference between mental fatigue and physical fatigue because both can affect motivation. Here is a thought experiment to help you better understand mental fatigue and why developing a strong mindset helps sustain performance.

There are two salespeople working in the same role, in the same company, and selling the same product. They both live alone, in the same condo building and have the same routine. They exercise at the same time, share the same hobbies, eat the same thing, and sleep well. They work on the same team, started at their company on the same day, and have the same target they need to hit.

Today they both exert the same amount of energy by calling the same number of leads and experience the same level of success and failure. They also each have deals expected to close at 3 p.m. today. Then at 3 p.m., one deal is won, and the other deal is lost.

Which rep will be more motivated?

You would be right to assume the rep whose deal closed would feel more motivated, but too often we confuse motivation with physical energy. They are not the same. The fatigue felt after losing a deal is not physical. It's mental.

Motivation comes from perceiving progress (deal closing), which releases dopamine in the brain and suppresses our desire to give up or quit. When a deal we were expecting to close is lost, dopamine plummets, and so does our motivation.

This is why adopting a growth mindset and being able to reframe a challenge as a positive is so important. They help us perceive failure as learning, growth, and progress, which limits the drop in dopamine and keeps you motivated to keep selling. A great book all salespeople should read to help develop these growth mindset skills is Carol Dweck's *Mindset: The New Psychology of Success*.

FEBRUARY, Day 28: Two Tennis Balls and a Sock

Using two tennis balls and a sock to stretch my neck is one of my favorite self-care strategies. Sounds weird, but let me explain by asking you a question: What's normally the first thing you do when you get off a long-haul flight? You stretch. Stretching helps reset your body and release the buildup of physical stress it incurred from being put in an environment it's not built to be in, like being trapped on a plane with no leg room for five hours or more.

Unfortunately many of us are working in comparable environments every single day but not managing our physical stress effectively. Even in the most ergonomically designed workspaces, the human body is not designed to sit and look at a screen for seven to eight hours per day. For me, my body responds to this type of physical stress by leaning my head forward, tightening my shoulders, and compressing the area between the top of my neck and the base of my skull. Left untreated, this stress response can often turn into some nasty tension headaches or migraines.

Enter the two-tennis-balls-and-a-sock strategy, which is a solution that was recommended by my physiotherapist. Simply put two tennis balls (lacrosse balls are too hard) in a sock and tie the sock shut. Then lie on your back and roll out the area at the base of your skull and the top of your neck. Complete this exercise two minutes before work, two minutes at lunch, two minutes after work, and two minutes before bed. It has worked like magic, and maybe it will do the same for you.

Similar to stretching before and after a long-haul flight, this strategy has helped prepare my body for a long working day and offload the buildup of physical stress before it gets too high. For the data lovers reading this, I use a WHOOP to track my recovery score (essentially a data point on overall stress levels), and I usually hover around 65%. When I first started following this neck rolling cadence every day for a week, which was the only thing I changed in my routine, my average recovery score increased to 84%, meaning my body was primed for peak performance each day.

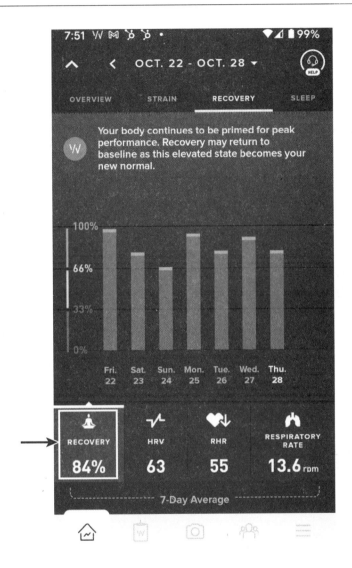

FEBRUARY, Day 29: When You're Not 100%

You won't be 100% every day. You might not even feel 50% today. That's okay. When you or the people around you are feeling this way, you have to remember three things: When everyone is looking left, you go right. When everyone is distracted, you have an opportunity to thrive. When everyone is paralyzed by fear, you have an opportunity to move.

Even if you're moving at 50% and things are not perfect, this is your moment. In a world that is in a constant state of change and dominated by fear, it will never be easier than it is right now to stand out from your peers, colleagues, and competitors. It's a time when you can truly help people and make yourself irreplaceable.

Show yourself some self-compassion. It's okay to be nervous, fearful, and depressed during these uncertain times in the world, but you need to block out distractions. Remember, everyone is looking left and what they're seeing is making them panic. They want something better to look at but can't find it. Today you just need to take that one slow step right. Then another and another and another . . .

Give them a reason to look right, and all eyes will be on you. Focus on completing that one thing you don't feel like doing but will help you show up a better version of yourself tomorrow.

FEBRUARY, Day 30: How to End Stigmas

I was fortunate to test positive for COVID for the first time two years into the pandemic. It was relatively mild, but during the experience I couldn't stop thinking about how great a lesson it was in stigma and the power of normalizing experiences.

As soon as I tested positive, I grabbed my phone and messaged everyone I had seen recently to tell them. I didn't think twice. Everyone I messaged responded: "I had COVID three months ago—you got this." "My friend just got COVID last week." "How are you feeling? Can I help?" Then it hit me; how different would this experience have been for me and my friends at the start of the pandemic? It would have been:

- Scary;
- Uncomfortable;
- Upsetting;
- Embarrassing;
- Shameful;
- Nervous;
- Threatening;
- Humiliating.

Hell, who knows if I would have had the courage to even tell them? This is how uncomfortable emotions created by stigma prevent important conversations from taking place, which affects the health of individuals and the group over time.

The good news is the pandemic has provided an amazing playbook to end COVID stigma, which can be used to effectively end stigmas in other areas of our life such as those tied to mental health. Ending a stigma requires thousands of micro-conversations that:

- Create awareness;
- Educate;
- Provide data;
- Offer solutions;
- Share experiences.

This is how we normalize a challenging experience in which people feel safe to share what they're going through and feel confident they have the resources to cope. Normalization is the antidote to stigma, and normalization requires *consistency*. If you're a leader, I encourage you to share your challenging experiences with your team and discuss resources or articles that create awareness, educate, provide data, and/or offer solutions on a regular basis. Start doing what's required to end mental health stigma and watch your team culture, health, and performance flourish.

FEBRUARY, Day 31: The Date Jar

Are you having a stressful week and need something to look forward to? Try implementing a date jar.

Our brains are anticipation machines and planning something you can look forward to every week is an easy way to keep motivation and well-being high during a busy work week. When we anticipate something we're really looking forward to such as an upcoming vacation, going to a concert, or a friend's birthday, dopamine is released in the brain. This release in dopamine can be so powerful that we can actually enjoy thinking about the upcoming event more than enjoying the actual event itself.

Usually thinking of a fun activity to plan and look forward to is the toughest part, but my girlfriend and I have made this process easier by using a date jar. Anytime we think of a fun idea, see a restaurant we want to try, or a new event in the city that excites us, we write it on a piece of paper and put it in the date jar. You can get really creative with this and include things such as: "Get off at a random subway stop and explore the area around it." Or "Organize a Hot Wings challenge or trivia night with friends." Every Sunday, we each pull a date from the jar and decide on the one we like the best. This ensures we plan time together, while giving us something to look forward to every week.

The best part is you also don't need a significant other to try this strategy and it might be a fun idea to implement with your sales team or best friend at work.

FEBRUARY, Day 32: Who's More Responsible?

Who's more responsible for employee mental health, the salesperson or the company? This question is easy to answer when we look at the physical conditioning of athletes in sports.

Physical conditioning is the process in which an athlete's body is prepared to achieve peak performance, build resilience to stressors, and improve recovery times. This conditioning process involves intentional attempts by *both* athletes and teams to improve the physical health of individuals through various fitness programs. Every pro sports organization on the planet recognizes that they will never be able to win without having a team of highly conditioned athletes and a world-class fitness program. That's why they take responsibility and do things such as:

- Talk about physical fitness regularly;
- Teach athletes about the importance of physical conditioning;
- Provide access to equipment, tools, trainers, and experts;
- Run drills and practice physical conditioning regularly;
- Set achievable goals;
- Collect consistent athlete feedback;
- Measure and track the physical health of their athletes daily;
- Adapt programs to athlete body types;
- Adapt programs to athlete positions;
- Allocate adequate time to recover from stress;
- Mitigate high-risk scenarios where athletes can get hurt.

Athletes are responsible for having some understanding of physical health (top athletes have invested in learning more than the rest), but their main responsibility is to train and engage in the items above on a consistent basis. If athletes regularly make bad choices such as skip practice, neglect sleep, party all night, eat junk, and don't put in the effort to condition their body, then they're not holding up their end of the bargain. They're letting the organization down and deserve to be traded or fired.

The answer to our initial question will become pretty clear if you go back and swap the words above like "athlete" with "salesperson" and "physical conditioning/fitness" with "mental conditioning/fitness." Most companies are doing hardly any of the conditioning best practices above, even though many are free to implement. Sure, you could argue salespeople are making bad choices, but the company has to show up for them first and set the standards for optimal mental health.

Knowledge workers are called "knowledge" workers because they're competing in a mental game. Expecting world-class performance from a sales team is just not realistic when companies and their leaders fail to lead by example.

FEBRUARY, Day 33: David vs Goliath

The small sales teams that were most successful during the COVID-19 pandemic realized that this was their moment to shine and saw it as an opportunity. Before the pandemic, their products were buried behind the million-dollar marketing budgets, massive workforces, and automation technology of much bigger competitors who had seemingly unlimited resources.

It was a David vs Goliath scenario.

But all of that changed for a brief moment in time when the pandemic hit. The rigid processes and massive workforces that were once an advantage became a cumbersome load to carry. They felt like heavy armor weighing down the slow-moving Goliaths of the world, who got stuck in the mud, a place they have never been before. The Goliaths could no longer think about winning because they were too focused on removing "extra weight" so they didn't sink.

But the small sales teams who shined during this time leaned into their inner David and were at home in the mud. They loved the mud. They were scrappy. They had the ability to be lean and adapt. They were creative. They were persistent. They were disciplined, and their authentic message could now shine through. The rapidly changing world played to their strengths, and they were proud of being a David. Davids found other Davids, and they rapidly built online communities to thrive in a new digitally connected world.

These lessons from this time in history cannot be forgotten. The world will continue to be an extremely uncertain, complex, and ambiguous environment. If you feel stuck today, stop thinking like a Goliath and how you can survive and instead start thinking more like a David who can thrive. Lean into your strengths, experiment with a new process, and reach out to others in your community who can help.

This is how you'll win.

FEBRUARY, Day 34: Rejection Handle

In sales, dating, and even in politics, rejection hurts. That's why we all need to have a rejection handle. This is a plan we can follow that will help us *respond* logically, rather than *react* emotionally. It helps us navigate the difficult emotions tied to rejection in a mentally healthy way and helps us remain positive.

Most salespeople will be familiar with the structure of a rejection handle because it follows the same structure as an objection handle used to handle buyer objections: If X happens, I say Y. If the buyer objects to price, I say, "Discussing price can always make people feel uneasy, especially on top of the change involved with implementing a new solution; however, you mentioned X was creating a lot of problems for Y. How expensive is that going to be if these issues don't get resolved?"

Plans like objection handles help us protect our performance, while feeling more calm and in control when facing an obstacle. Now we just need to create a different type of plan for when our emotions become an obstacle following the sting of a difficult rejection: "If I get rejected, I do Y." Below is an article outlining a rejection handle in detail and how you can build one for yourself. The examples are in the context of sales but will apply to many aspects of your life. Next time you're entering a situation where you may face rejection, make sure you map out a rejection handle beforehand.

 Scan here to learn how to build your first rejection handle.

FEBRUARY, Day 35: Dangerous Expectations

One of the most important lessons I had to learn is how destructive it can be when we lead with our expectations. When we're under high levels of stress, feeling burnt out, and our mental health is in decline, our emotional brain is in the driver seat. Our perspective shrinks, which means our self-protection system focuses only on serving ourselves and protecting our ego.

When this happens we start imposing our expectations on others. We *expect* buyers to respond to our "perfectly" crafted email. We *expect* buyers to be kind when we cold-call them. We *expect* buyers to want to buy our product after our demo. We *expect* friends, family, and loved ones to know what we need. We *expect* others to automatically perceive what we perceive.

Our ego wants to impose our expectations on the world so it can feel safe. When these expectations are not met, we typically react by adding more anger, frustration, and resentment to our relationships with others. You can prevent this from happening when you're mindful of your expectations.

Today, before entering into one of the many uncomfortable and high-stress situations that exist within sales, ask yourself, "What expectations of others are you leading with? Are they hurting you or helping you? How can you be more vulnerable and transparent with how you feel? How can you be more curious and compassionate to someone else's perspective?" This is how you take responsibility for your emotions and own your part in the relationship.

FEBRUARY, Day 36: You Need a Hobby

Do you have a hobby that helps you unplug from work? You need one if you want to maximize your recovery and perform your best each day.

A recent study of 10,000 tech workers who went remote found work hours increased by 30%, but productivity fell by 20%.[1] The study attributes the drop in performance to more interruptions, more meetings, less one-on-one time, and less coaching from supervisors.

I agree these factors play a *huge* role in decreasing performance, but when I read this study, my main concern was around why "hours worked" increased by 30%. My hypothesis is that very few of us have hobbies that we're passionate about. Feeling bored is an extremely uncomfortable emotion, and many of us respond to this emotion by reaching for our phone to scroll social media or watch Netflix in our spare time. After 10 minutes of finding no boredom relief, it's easy to think, "Well I may as well respond to that email from earlier." One email turns into two hours, which sets us up for a restless sleep and makes it impossible for us to perform our best the next day.

Hobbies are important because they relieve the discomfort you feel when you're bored. One of mine is playing a Marvel card game called Marvel Champions, which I bought at the start of the pandemic. I love it, and it has played a huge role in helping me unplug from work, get off screens, and recover from stress. Rather than working late tonight, lean into your nerdy side and find your hobby. No matter how uncool it may be.

FEBRUARY, Day 37: Do Wellness Initiatives Work?

Sales leaders can often be hesitant to invest into mental health and wellness initiatives for their teams. In my experience, the hesitation often comes from the uncertainty surrounding two primary questions: (1) Do wellness initiatives actually work at improving mental health in sales? (2) What impact will a wellness initiative have on my team?

According to the World Health Organization, the potential ROI from investing into better mental health support is huge. Their data showed every $1 invested into scaling up treatment for depression and anxiety leads to a $4 return in better health and ability to work.[2] There are also significant risks and downsides for companies who neglect mental health and wellness initiatives. For example, according to one recent survey, 70% of employees said they would quit if another employer offered better policies to reduce burnout.[3]

You might be thinking, "But those are average workplace numbers; what about sales specifically?" Well, in the "2021 State of Mental Health in Sales Report" we completed with UNCrushed and The Harris Consulting Group, we found a strong positive correlation between wellness initiatives and mental health. Among salespeople who felt strongly that their company was prioritizing burnout and wellness initiatives, 63% rated their mental health as good, very good, or excellent. This was over 2X higher than salespeople working at companies who felt like wellness and burnout initiatives were being neglected.

Within these sales organizations that were least focused on wellness and mental health, only 26% of salespeople rated their mental health as good or better.

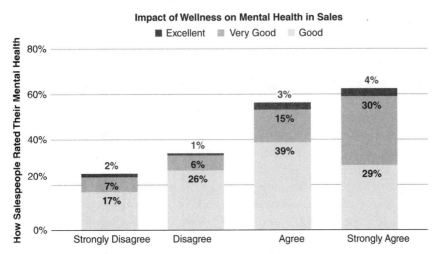

During the last 6 months - You felt like your company was actively prioritizing initiatives focused on Wellness & Burnout.

Image Source: T. Clarke, R. Harris, and J. Riseley. "2021 State of Mental Health in Sales Report." UNCrushed, Sales Health Alliance, The Harris Consulting Group. May 2021. https://theharrisconsultinggroup.com/state-of-mental-health-in-sales-report.

This connection between wellness initiatives and mental health is an important finding because data from this report also showed a correlation between mental health and sales performance. Among salespeople who rated their mental health as very good or excellent, 70% rated their sales performance as very good or excellent. This was over 3X higher than salespeople with the worst mental health, of whom only 22% rated their sales performance as very good or excellent.

Though we cannot claim causation with this data, there is a strong correlation between mental health and sales performance that shouldn't be overlooked. As mental health improves, sales performance increases significantly, which is why mental health deserves a seat at the table when sales organizations are determining revenue generating priorities.

FEBRUARY, Day 38: Save Past Experiences

If you're new to sales, your first few days, weeks, and even months leading up to closing your first sale will be extremely challenging. That's why you need to make sure you *save* the experience of closing your first sale after it happens.

When we're operating in a new environment such as sales, where the perceived risk of failure and uncertainty is high, your anxiety will be higher than normal. This is because your brain has not yet acquired the stories and past experiences it needs to remain confident and feel safe in the face of sales adversity. One reason salespeople become more resilient over time is because the more experience you have, the more evidence your brain has to combat negative thinking.

For example, when a tenured sales rep gets hung up on, they subconsciously *insert* a past experience of closing the next person. If they find themselves behind target, they *insert* a past experience of rallying from behind. When they miss their target, they *insert* a past experience of bouncing back.

As a new rep, you can speed up this natural hardening process by making it easier for your brain to save and recall your early stories of success in sales. After you close your first sale, take 10 minutes to capture that story. Write down everything you had to endure and what you overcame to get to that point. *Save* it for later and reread it on days when self-doubt and anxiety come knocking after a few bad beats. It will be easier to combat negative thinking by keeping this story visible because the proof is right in front of you.

FEBRUARY, Day 39: Responding to Good News

If someone on your team shares with you that they just closed a *big* deal that they had been working on for weeks, what do you think is the best way to respond? Here are six options to consider based on research by psychology professor Shelly Gable, from the University of California[4]:

1. **Active destructive:** You belittle the news.
    Example: "You just got lucky on that one. Plus working with that client long term is going to cause you a lot of stress."
2. **Passive destructive:** You ignore the news and shift focus to yourself.
    Example: "That's nice. I just closed the biggest deal in company history!"
3. **Passive:** You barely acknowledge the news.
    Example: "Nice!"

It should be clear that you definitely should *avoid* responding to your peers in any of these ways and instead respond in one of the following three ways.

---

4. **Passive constructive:** You acknowledge their good news and support them but schedule a better time to discuss in detail.
    Example: "That's so exciting to hear that deal closed. I'm really busy at the moment, but can you tell me more about it later? I really want to hear what happened."
5. **Active constructive:** You immediately support them and ask questions.
    Example: "That's *amazing* news! Tell me everything! How did it all go down?"
6. **Recognition:** You recognize and celebrate someone's accomplishments before they tell you.
    Example: "I saw how much effort you put into trying to implement the feedback I gave you on your pitch. Keep practicing because you're definitely getting better."

Sales can feel pretty lonely at times. Especially when we've encountered a few deals or calls that didn't bounce our way. By responding in a constructive fashion or by recognizing the efforts of others, you play an active role in building a more supportive work environment. More importantly, you capitalize on these positive moments in times where you and your peers can both improve your well-being by hearing and discussing some good news.

FEBRUARY, Day 40: Changing Jobs

If you think about why some salespeople change jobs, it becomes pretty clear as to why it's important for sales organizations to start the mental health conversation during new hire onboarding. In the interview process, managers want to believe what they hear and they want to believe salespeople are leaving jobs because of standard reasons such as:

- Lack of recognition;
- Lack of career growth;
- Opportunity for more money;
- More flexibility;
- Better perks;
- Better location;
- More meaningful purpose.

But in reality there are likely going to be salespeople who are hired and have left their previous job as a result of more serious issues that never come up in the interview process such as:

- Toxic environments;
- Abusive bosses;
- Bullying and discrimination;
- Burnout, anxiety, and/or depression;
- Insomnia;
- Addiction and/or unhealthy coping habits.

Depending on the severity of these issues and the length of time someone has been trying to get out of an unsafe working environment, it's *very* possible that a new hire may be dealing with trauma, self-esteem issues, limiting beliefs, and ongoing mental health struggles that carry over. It's unlikely that these more serious issues are going to magically disappear in the two weeks they have off between leaving their old job and starting their new role.

This is why it's important for organizations to start the mental health conversation on day one. They need to highlight the employee assistance program (EAP) and mental health services they have invested into so new hires know how to start using them immediately upon starting. In addition to these programs, new sales hires can benefit from mental health, resilience, and stress-management training as part of onboarding.

This type of toolkit equips sellers with the tools they need to navigate unique stressors they face in sales and empowers sellers to take a preventative approach to issues such as burnout so they have less of an impact on sales performance in the future.

 If you're curious to see the online program I've built for sellers that give them a toolkit like the one mentioned above, then scan here.

FEBRUARY Endnotes

1. Vincent, I. "Remote workers put in longer hours but were less efficient, study says."*New York Post.*June 12, 2021. https://nypost.com/2021/06/12/remote-workers-put-in-longer-hours-but-were-less-efficient-study/.
2. "Investing in treatment for depression and anxiety leads to fourfold return." World Health Organization. April 13, 2016. https://www.who.int/news/item/13-04-2016-investing-in-treatment-for-depression-and-anxiety-leads-to-fourfold-return.
3. "When Vacations Aren't Enough: New Visier Survey Finds 70% of Burnt Out Employees Would Leave Current Job." Visier. https://www.visier.com/blog/new-survey-70-percent-burnt-out-employees-would-leave-current-job/.
4. Gable, S., Reis, H., Impett, E., and Asher, E. "What Do You Do When Things Go Right? The Intrapersonal and Interpersonal Benefits of Sharing Positive Events." *Journal of Personality and Social Psychology* 2004, Vol 87, No. 2, 228–245.

MARCH

MARCH, Day 41: "Grinding" in Sales

The definition of "grind" (verb): *Reduce something to small particles or powder by crushing it.*

We could replace "something" with "a salesperson," and the definition feels *way* too familiar to "grinding" in sales. We as a sales community need to rethink what it means to "grind" in sales because the way it's used today is not healthy. Learning about "The Story of Two Woodcutters" can help us reframe the sales grind; the story goes something like this:

There are two lumberjacks who spend all day cutting wood. They exert the same energy, use the same technique, follow the same process, and use the same type of ax. But every day, the same lumberjack cuts more wood than the other one. The only difference? The lumberjack who cuts more wood "disappears" at lunchtime for an hour each day. Frustrated by this, the lumberjack who is *working harder* and *grinding* approaches the more successful lumberjack when they return from lunch and ask, "How do you cut more wood than me? I'm working an hour longer than you every single day!" The successful lumberjack pauses, smiles and says, "I go home at lunch to sharpen my ax."

The moral of the story for salespeople and leaders is our mind and our mental health is our ax. If you're grinding it every single day on a piece of "wood" at work, then you need to stop waiting until it gets "dull" or breaks before taking time to sharpen it. Sharpening your mind and mental health requires daily attention and leads to better performance.

MARCH, Day 42: Fight Together, Not Alone

When small companies are running out of cash-flow and runway, every sales leader should be having a difficult heart-to-heart conversation with their sales team. The type of conversation where leaders honestly tell the reps on their team three key things: What are the minimum deliverables needed at the team level for everyone to keep their job? How will they be financially supported during this process? And how much runway or time do they have left to achieve the team deliverables? Some sales leaders may disagree with this approach and think this type of candor will only create more frenzy and panic, but this isn't true. Leaders have to realize that radical transparency is the only way forward in trying times.

As a leader, you owe it to your sales team to give them a chance to fight. If you leave them in the dark guessing, team uncertainty will undoubtedly become team anxiety. When sales reps are uncertain about their job security, the ability to afford basic necessities such as food and shelter are perceived as at risk. They'll be in survival mode and contemplating whether they should *fight* for their current company or *flight* toward other companies or methods to support themselves and their families.

Give your team a chance to fight as a whole rather than trying to be a leader who has to fight alone. Radical transparency will build trust, bring people together, and allow emotions to calm down during a critical moment in time when team goals need to be aligned. Only then will the creative and logical parts of the brain reactivate in your team, and the group as a whole will have a fighting chance to succeed.

MARCH, Day 43: Motivation Bucket Checklist

At the start of a new month or quarter, sales leaders can become anxious and start to panic if their team (or team member) is not motivated out of the gate. The answer to reengaging your unmotivated sales reps lies in one of these six buckets:

1. **They're bored, and sales tasks have become meaningless.**
   Solution: Help them make work more purposeful by showing them how the actions they are taking today are making an impact in the lives of customers and the people around them.
2. **There is internal conflict between teammates.**
   Solution: Bring the reps together so they can find common ground and move past the conflict.
3. **The team is upset with you, and you just don't know it.**
   Solution: Reflect on your behavior as a leader; did you do or say something that could have been misperceived by the team? If so, then you need to apologize, clarify, and show compassion by taking the team's perspective into account.
4. **They're burnt out and exhausted from the last month.**
   Solution: Give them a day off to prioritize self-care activities they don't normally have time for.
5. **They perceive their target as too challenging, and they're feeling helpless.**
   Solution: Break the target down into smaller, achievable daily goals. Work with them to develop a plan and explain how you'll support them in achieving their target.
6. **They are dealing with a personal issue outside of work that is distracting them.**
   Solution: Ask them if they are okay, and ask them what they need from you to support them through this challenging time.

If you're an individual sales rep and you're feeling unmotivated today, you can also run through this checklist to help uncover what's holding you back. The more in tune you are with tending to these six areas, the more consistent your motivation will be each day.

MARCH, Day 44: Meaningful Work in Sales

Meaningful work has long been connected to improvements in well-being and performance metrics, but determining how meaningful work is to you can be difficult. One way you can do this is by answering this question: "If financially secure, would you continue with your current line of work even if you were no longer paid?"

If you answered "No" to this question, then a simple way to make work more meaningful is to challenge your current perspective of "work," which you need to deconstruct. The best way to do this is to draw a line down the center of a piece of paper and on one side of the page start making a list of all your daily tasks. For salespeople, these tasks might include actions such as making 50 calls, running a demo, updating the CRM, having a one-on-one with my manager, etc. Then, once you've completed your list, on the other side of the line answer this question for each task you've written down: "Why am I doing this?" What you'll find by answering this question is your answers will likely fall into one of two buckets:

Bucket 1: Driven by Insecurity.
 Example: Attaining power, status, money, self-esteem, appearance or popularity.

Bucket 2: Driven by Growth.
 Example: Achieving mastery, self-improvement, creativity, genuinely serving/helping others, or making greater contributions to society.

For each task that is driven by insecurity, you then want to challenge the motivator (the why) behind each task and brainstorm how you can challenge your beliefs, attitudes, and opinions toward that task to be more growth focused. For example, rather than perceiving a task such as making 50 dials as a metric you need to hit to keep your job, think of it as getting 50 opportunities to connect with new potential customers who are struggling with a problem you can help solve. This is how you rebuild your perception of work with more growth-focused tasks, which in turn will make it feel more meaningful as a whole.

MARCH, Day 45: Connecting through Failure

"I feel like a failure, and I'm just not cut out for sales." How do you respond to this statement from a rep as a sales leader? In my experience, most leaders will try their best and respond in the following ways:

"C'mon, you know that's not true."

"You've hit your target 10 times in a row."

"Remember that big client you just closed."

"You're gonna close the next one."

"Don't worry about it. I believe in you."

"Just focus on more volume."

If you're a leader and have tried any of the statements above, you've likely been frustrated by how ineffective they are at helping your rep feel better. You think, "I'm being so positive and supportive; why isn't it helping?"

It's not helping because you're trying to respond to an *emotional* statement from the rep with a *rational* answer. When you try to talk an emotional rep into being more rational, it will likely make them shut down further. It subconsciously conveys that you as their leader do not understand what they're feeling. This can make them feel more isolated and lonely. So what do you do instead? Try saying, "I appreciate you sharing. I know what it feels like to feel like a failure in sales. It happened to me when . . ." Then go on to open up and share a personal story about a time when you felt like a failure by answering these questions:

What happened that made you feel like a failure?

How did feeling like a failure make you feel?

How did others help you?

What actions made you feel better?

Your job as a leader is *not* to tell a rep how they should be feeling. Your job is to help them understand that what they are feeling is normal. You do this by building an emotional connection through a shared experience. That way the rep you're helping knows you get what it feels like to be in their shoes. This creates safety from fears of blame or judgment, so you can both work through what the rep is feeling together. Only when fear is removed can rational conversations begin.

MARCH, Day 46: The Problem with Rewards

Before sales leaders decide to run another sales contest or start playing around with commission structures to "boost" motivation, we need to look at what the data tells us about rewards. Rewards absolutely motivate people, but they only motivate people to get the reward. This has long-term consequences, and research on rewards found in Alfie Kohn's book *Punished by Rewards* tell us[1]:

1. Rewards get you quantity but not quality;
2. The bigger the reward, the easier the task people choose;
3. You need to keep offering more rewards;
4. Rewards cause people to make more mistakes;
5. Rewards cause people to take less risks;
6. Rewards make people less creative;
7. Rewards make it harder to learn;
8. Rewards make leaders less patient;
9. Rewards do not resolve underlying behavior issues;
10. Rewards perpetuate individualism over teamwork;
11. Using rewards is a form of manipulation (one person controlling the other);
12. Providing *no* rewards works better.

If using a reward to improve performance has all of these negative side effects, then why are they used so often in sales? They're used because it's easy to do and they trick sales leaders into thinking they work when they see the quantity (not quality) in metrics going up. Offering rewards also distracts leaders from having difficult conversations around *why* sales performance is actually suffering, such as uncomfortable conversations about burnout, mental health, diversity, and relationship issues that are creating toxicity and eroding the foundation of sales team culture.

Sales leaders need to stop assuming why a sales team is underperforming and need to stop opting for the easy route of providing a reward. Instead, they need to ask the hard questions and be willing to listen to answers they may not want to hear.

MARCH, Day 47: Pattern Interrupts

"Pattern interrupt" is my new favorite mental health term. Just like a pattern interrupt can be used during a cold call to break the pattern of someone saying "No" to a sales pitch, they can also be used to break the pattern of a downward spiral.

Our brains and bodies love patterns, habits, and routines because they allow us to unconsciously execute behaviors at a lower energy cost. Unfortunately, many of us get stuck in negative thought patterns throughout the day that affect our mental health and ability to perform our best. This is when a pattern interrupt can be extremely helpful in breaking the pattern of how you're thinking or feeling. Here are some examples:

- HIIT workout;
- Wim Hof breathing;
- Cold shower;
- Gratitude;
- Yoga;
- Meditation.

These are all actions we can use to interrupt a negative thought pattern by engaging our mind and body in an unexpected way that helps us unstick from the negative thoughts cycling in through our heads.

The most challenging part of a pattern interrupt is actually using them when we need them. We won't want to meditate, work out, or jump in some cold water when we're stuck in a thought pattern that has us feeling hopeless, defeated, or negative about ourselves and the world around us. Label this as a pattern you have the opportunity to change. Take an action to interrupt the pattern of a downward spiral, and change your mood.

MARCH, Day 48: Steve Kerr

Sales leaders, if you're trying to lower burnout in your sales teams, then start asking yourself: What would Steve Kerr do?

For those who don't know, Steve Kerr is the coach of the Golden State Warriors and responsible for the best shooter in NBA history—Steph Curry. Formerly a dynasty and championship team, the Golden State Warriors had some bad luck with injuries at the end of the 2019 season. Much like a sales team, they still had fans and customers to please, with metrics to hit in the short term. But unlike a sales team, Steve Kerr and the organization were committed to playing the long game, which meant putting the health of players first.

When the Warriors roster was heavily depleted in 2019, Steve Kerr said, "We're not throwing Steph out there for 40 minutes to chase wins. We've got another game tomorrow. We want Steph to be playing at a high level for many years, so we're going to stay disciplined and try to keep him at that 34–35-minute mark." As a result of this long term strategy and protecting player health, they went on to win the NBA championship in 2022.

Sales leaders, if your team is injured, experiencing burnout, or people are foregoing some much needed vacation time, it's your job to manage your players' minutes in a healthy way. Like the Warriors, you have another game and target next month. Stop chasing short-term wins at the expense of your people. Your customers want to work with people who are performing their best.

MARCH, Day 49: Am I Experiencing Burnout?

Burnout is a popular topic these days, but most of the articles you read online aren't very effective in helping you determine if you're experiencing it. That's because experiencing burnout is not black-or-white, or something you either have or don't have.

It's more nuanced than that, and instead, burnout happens along a spectrum. In order to determine where you fall on a burnout spectrum, you need to evaluate changes in your thoughts, feelings, and behaviors based on three key factors:

- Intensity;
- Frequency;
- Duration.

Much like a burn victim who has degrees of skin burn, most of us are dealing with various degrees of burnout, which affect performance more and more as they get worse. For example, feeling burnt out after two weeks of end-of-quarter stress is way different than someone experiencing chronic stress after working in a toxic environment for two years.

To help you truly understand your burnout levels, I've written an article and have created a free burnout calculator (near the end of the article) that will give you a much better indicator of how you're doing overall.

 Access the Free Burnout Calculator by scanning here.

MARCH, Day 50: What Are We Doing?

If you hit your target, you will be *rewarded* with a commission check, but if you miss your target, you will be *punished* with a PIP. No matter how you slice it, either situation results in a company or sales leader "doing something to" a sales rep. Both ways try to maintain control over a sales rep's behavior using extrinsic rewards or fear of punishment, as if we're training a new pet to behave a certain way. This is dehumanizing.

We need to stop leaning so heavily on rewards or punishments and instead find ways to intrinsically motivate our teams so sales tasks become more enjoyable, creative, and done out of a sales rep's own free will.

This means leaders have to spend more time helping sales reps connect their own personal goals, values, and morals to the vision, goals, and core values of a company. Sales reps and companies have to be aligned and connected to each other through more than just a paycheck. Real motivation and perseverance comes from being emotionally connected to your work; it's a core building block toward mental resilience. Not the carrots we're chasing or stones we're trying to avoid.

MARCH, Day 51: Vulnerability Paradox

How likely are you to be vulnerable with someone who is judging your performance? The answer is probably very unlikely. This question highlights the Vulnerability Paradox, which exists in sales, and something else I learned while reading Alfie Kohn's book *Punished by Rewards.*[2]

A salesperson's performance is under the microscope and being judged on what they produce *every* single day. When a sales rep's performance *decreases*, judgment, pressure, and focus by their manager on outcomes *increases*. Logically, this natural instinct makes sense because many managers are incentivized to prioritize numbers over people and use rewards or punishment to drive performance. But therein lies the paradox.

If sales performance is being affected by anxiety, depression, burnout, or stressors inside and outside the workplace—things unlikely to be resolved by a reward or punishment—then discussing these challenges will require the rep to be open and vulnerable in how they communicate. However, the only time they feel safe to be vulnerable in sales is when they have the numbers. Under more scrutiny and judgment by the manager, defense mechanisms go up and performance issues remain.

To resolve this paradox, managers need to ensure sales performance outcomes are their *secondary* focus. Only when mental health and well-being become their *primary* focus can peak sales team performance be achieved through vulnerable conversations that resolve underlying performance issues.

MARCH, Day 52: Revenge Bedtime Procrastination

I recently found out about a new term called "revenge bedtime procrastination." This is when you stubbornly stay up late for no good reason at the expense of sleep. According to the research on revenge bedtime procrastination, it happens for a few reasons[3]:

1. Revenge for having no "me" time during the day;
2. Feeling lonely and scrolling social media;
3. Avoidance of our thoughts and emotions because they scare us.

Essentially it's our body trying to meet unfulfilled needs in an unhealthy way. The best way I've found to combat this bad habit is to do the following steps. First, decide when you're going to stop working, *before* you start working. Second, stick to a strict shutdown routine (~45 min.) of self-care at the end of your workday. Put it on your calendar.

During your shutdown routine you want to focus on addressing the neglected area above that might cause you to procrastinate going to bed later in the evening. For example, no "me" time? Play, garden, exercise, or do something you really enjoy that is not work related. Feeling lonely? Call a friend while you take a walk outside. Avoiding emotions? Journal about what you're feeling and label the individual emotions that you're struggling with.

Scan here to access an exercise that will help you with your journaling practice so you can sort through the emotions that are keeping you up at night.

MARCH, Day 53: Not Programmed to Exercise

Are you having trouble exercising while working remotely? You're not alone, and this is primarily because humans did not evolve to work out. This perspective was shared recently by Harvard professor Daniel Lieberman, who specializes in human evolution and biology. The key point he makes is that physical activity is different from exercise[4].

When you look at human history, our ancestors spent a substantial amount of time each day doing physical activities such as hunting, gathering, and protecting their tribe. These were involuntary physical activities required of the body in order to stay safe, stay strong, and survive. Given the limited resources at the time and physical demand of these tasks, we evolved to conserve our energy and *avoid* voluntary activities that would burn extra calories; exercise is a *voluntary* activity.

Today, resources are abundant, and the daily physical activity required to survive has declined. Our body evolved to sit on the couch watching Netflix because it's programmed to conserve energy. We are not programmed to voluntarily work out, which means we often skip our daily exercise and miss all the amazing mental health benefits it provides.

You can fight your natural urge to sit on the couch by connecting exercise to something bigger than yourself. It needs to be bigger than something you *should* do to be healthy. How will exercising today better the lives of not only yourself but also the people you care most deeply about? Think about your kids, clients, colleagues, and partners—how will it help *them*.

MARCH, Day 54: Sales Is a Marathon

Sales is a marathon and not a sprint. But the entire sales industry is trying to sprint a marathon that never ends. When you try to force people to sprint a marathon, people get hurt and people are going to burn out.

A better way to do this became clear when my girlfriend was training for a marathon and walked me through her process. I asked her, how do you run 42 km without getting hurt leading up to the race? She explained her training schedule went something like this: One week she would run 16 km, the next week would be 14 km. Then she would run 20 km and the following week she would run 16 km. Then she would run 24 km, followed by a 20 km run the next week. This is a process endurance athletes use to ensure they balance the incremental stress of longer distances with the appropriate rest and recovery to limit the risk of injury.

Sales teams need to learn to treat sales like a marathon. Rather than trying to sprint further and further distances each month or quarter, sales leaders can use the endurance methodology outlined above to set sales targets that don't burn people out. Stretch sales targets should always be followed by a lower target to allow for recovery, reflection, and learning so peak sales performance can be sustained over the long term. If we just keep adding more stress, salespeople eventually break down.

MARCH, Day 55: Stoicism and Resilience

We can learn a lot about mental resilience from the Stoics, who are masters in managing uncomfortable emotions such as fear, loneliness, and grief. Below are my top two rules from the list of "50 Short Rules From the Stoics," which Ryan Holliday recently compiled[5]:

1. **Meditate on your mortality every day.**

    Thankfully my experience with testicular cancer in 2018 was not life threatening, because I caught it early, but it certainly woke me up to the fact that in another life I may not have been so lucky. While waiting for various test results throughout the process, it was the first time in my life that I seriously considered the answers to questions such as: "What if I only had a year left to live?" "How would I spend this time?" "What would I regret?" When you think about the answer to these questions, your priorities, purpose, and vision of what a meaningful life means to you becomes crystal clear. I recently passed the four-year cancer-free mark, and I still ask myself these questions daily to check that I'm still on the right path.

2. **Try to see the good in people.**

    The most emotional, angry, and stressful periods in our lives usually occur during interactions with other people when we feel wronged, slighted, judged, blamed, and defensive. These emotions can cloud our judgment and narrow our perception if we're not careful. Remembering to step back and challenge our initial assessments of people by trying to see the good in the other person is one of the best ways we can regain perspective.

MARCH, Day 56: Burnout and Control

Burnout is caused less by the amount of work we have to do and more about how controlled and powerless we feel in trying to complete our work. If you don't believe me, check out this data from the mental health survey we ran with UNCrushed and The Harris Consulting Group.

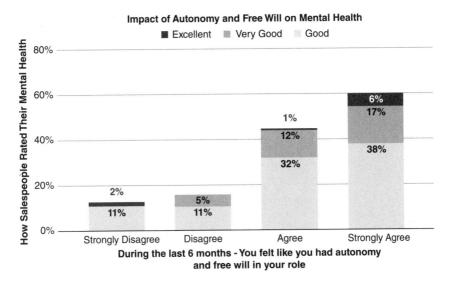

Image Source: T. Clarke, R. Harris, J. Riseley. "2021 State of Mental Health in Sales Report." UNCrushed, Sales Health Alliance, The Harris Consulting Group. May 2021. https://theharrisconsultinggroup.com/state-of-mental-health-in-sales-report.

Our data showed a strong positive correlation between autonomy and how salespeople rated their mental health. The more strongly salespeople agreed that they felt they had autonomy and free will in their role, the better they rated their mental health.

Among salespeople who strongly agreed they felt like they had autonomy and free will in their role, 61% rated their mental health as good, very good, or excellent. When salespeople strongly disagreed they felt they had autonomy and free will in their role, only 13% rated their mental health as good, very good, or excellent. Therefore, salespeople who feel strongly that they have autonomy and free will in their role are over 4.5 times more likely to rate their mental health as good or better, compared to salespeople who have no autonomy or free will in their role.

Part of improving mental health in sales means allowing reps more freedom to be creative during the sales process. If you're a sales leader, reflect on this question today: How are you empowering your team with more freedom and control in their day-to-day life? Maybe this means allowing more customization to be used within email templates? Or maybe it means allowing them to find creative ways to target prospects such as organizing a webinar? Whatever more autonomy and creativity looks like for the reps on your team, it's important, so make it a priority going forward.

MARCH, Day 57: "Squeezing" Salespeople

One of my biggest pet peeves is when sales leaders "squeeze" their reps. If you don't know what that means, it goes something like this:

Sales leader: "Everyone update your pipeline! We need to have accurate forecasts!"

Sales rep: "No problem—I'll get right on that."

Sales rep honestly and truthfully updates their pipeline.

Two weeks later at the start of a new month or quarter, the sales leader thinks: "Who can I squeeze this month?"

Sales leader proceeds to cherry-pick the reps with the healthiest pipeline forecasts and then blindsides them by dropping a massive quota on them.

This is the same sales leader who then complains that their sales reps cannot forecast correctly and wonders why they have:

- Disengaged and stressed-out reps;
- A toxic culture;
- Team trust issues;
- A retention problem.

Sales leader, I'm here to tell you that you are the problem. You are the one who cannot forecast. Stop rewarding good pipeline management with blindsides, chaos, and a whip. Let reps who manage their pipeline correctly crush it, make some good money, and take some time off to rest and recover.

MARCH, Day 58: Formula 1

Sales enablement teams should emulate Formula 1 car companies in their hunt for higher sales performance and efficiency. This is because they are currently forgetting about two key areas in their "enablement" process.

When you envision a Formula 1 race and you think about a Ferrari racing around the track, what do you see? You see a multimillion-dollar car with the best car technology in the world. In sales this is your tech stack, which is composed of all the best sales technologies on the market. You also see a driver who is being fed insight from their team on the sideline. This is your salesperson who is receiving training and coaching from their manager. But sales enablement usually stops there and are missing the following:

1. **Resilience:**
   Practical strategies the driver and salesperson can use to respond to stressful situations (near-death experiences or missing target). Tools that protect their mental health and keep performance high.
2. **Recovery:**
   Time off between races or quarters, when drivers and salespeople can recover from the stress of competition. This also includes pit stops during the race or quarter that keep the driver, car and salesperson from breaking down. Oftentimes, salespeople are never allowed to get off the track, and when enablement teams forget about these two areas, a sales team will never reach peak levels of performance that remain consistent over the long term.

MARCH, Day 59: My Team "Looks" Healthy

It's very easy to think you don't have a mental health problem with your sales team, just like it's easy to think a skinny person with high blood pressure doesn't need to go to the gym, because they look healthy.

More so than the body, the mind is very good at hiding when it's out of shape or injured. The mind can use deceptive defense mechanisms to keep other people out. Behind the forced smiles, the "I'm fine," and over-the-top ego or narcissism is a voice that is whispering, "I need help,"

A whisper that is lost behind the emotional intensity of rejection, failure of missing a target, machine-like sales metrics, and excessive partying.

It's up to sales leaders to give room on the sales floor for these whispers to be heard, a place where inner conflict can be resolved so superior outer sales performance can be achieved. We have to collectively move away from the leadership practice of burning and churning sales talent, while short-term revenue numbers get prioritized over mental health. The longer leaders wait to create safe spaces for these whispers to be heard, the more damage that gets done.

Sales leaders, a great starting place is to carve out time on your calendar for weekly mental health office hours. These are different from weekly one-on-ones that focus on performance. Let your team know that every week at a set time you'll be available for drop-ins if they need a place to talk openly, be vulnerable, or get something off their chest. In a remote world, this "place" can be an open video conference link they can drop into.

MARCH, Day 60: Mindful Eating

Do you often eat your meals while scrolling on your phone, at your desk working, or while in front of the TV? You need to stop doing this because you're missing out on one of the most enjoyable experiences life offers: tasting your food.

Hunger, like sex drive, is one of the most well-developed systems in our body that is highly connected to our emotions and nervous system. We can plug into this system through our tongue, which has on average between 2,000 and 8,000 taste buds, which help us experience our food. However, the problem is that we rarely use this system to our advantage. We're so busy watching cat videos, playing with our phones, or responding to emails while we eat, that we forget to focus on tasting our food.

Today, make a point to reconnect with this tasting experience. When you eat your meals, focus all your attention on the thousands of sensations you're tasting. Be curious and mystified by the fact that within each bite, millions of nutrients are entering your body to refuel your energy. Be grateful for the work that went into transporting ingredients from all over the world and the love that went into assembling your meal. We all know satisfying our hunger feels good, but actually tasting our food has the power to ground us. In doing so, we can temporarily shut off our anxious minds and experience the extreme pleasure and happiness food has to offer.

MARCH Endnotes

1. Kohn, A. (1999). *Punished by Rewards: The trouble with gold stars, incentive plans, A's, praise and other bribes.* Houghton Mifflin (Trade).
2. Ibid.
3. Singer, J. "'Revenge Bedtime Procrastination' Is Real, According to Psychologists." *Glamour.* January 28, 2021. https://www.glamour.com/story/revenge-bedtime-procrastination-is-real-according-to-psychologists.
4. Howse, L. "Humans have not evolved to exercise, says Harvard prof." CBC Radio. February 9, 2021. https://www.cbc.ca/radio/thecurrent/the-current-for-feb-9-2021-1.5906730/humans-have-not-evolved-to-exercise-says-harvard-prof-1.5907580.
5. Holiday, R. "50 Short Rules For Life From The Stoics." Ryan Holiday Meditations On Strategy And Life. https://ryanholiday.net/50-short-rules-for-life-from-the-stoics/

APRIL

APRIL, Day 61: Messy Humans

If you know a sales leader who is treating their salespeople like a number or a cog in a machine, then you might want to share this with them. A recent survey found Canadians would switch to a lower-paying job for better mental health perks[1]:

> "Human resources firm Morneau Shepell found 60% of Canadian employees would leave their employer if they were offered less money but better support for personal well-being. This trend was even seen among the 51% who reported high financial stress."

Gone are the days when organizations could pay a salesperson well and expect them to perform regardless of how they're being treated. Sales leaders *love* efficiency, data, metrics, and predictable revenue because it's objective, emotionless, and clean. If each rep on their team does enough of X, then they can safely predict they'll get Y. When the machine underperforms, they can easily replace the "broken parts."

But sales leaders have gone too far. They are not programming a machine. They are trying to motivate and develop people so they can be successful. This requires creating a mess, discussing emotions, encouraging learning through failure, and supporting mental health. It means being okay with *not* being perfect, because humans are far from being perfect. Only then can leaders really start to learn how to support their team and their mental health.

APRIL, Day 62: Exercise for $25,000?

Yes, you've probably heard it a thousand times and you know exercise is good for us (yawn). Tell me something you don't know, right?

Well, did you know exercise might make you feel as good as people earning $25,000 more than you? According to new research by Yale and Oxford on 1.2 million Americans, that is exactly what they found.[2] "Physically active people feel just as good as those who don't do sports but who earn about $25,000 more a year." In addition to the benefit in happiness, they found those who exercise also feel less bad throughout the year. The study showed that inactive people feel bad on average 18 more days a year, compared to their active counterparts.

As we all know, the hardest part of exercising is getting started. When we're tired it's usually the first thing we skip and default to more comfortable habits. To help you break this pattern, I have a three-day mini challenge for you: Plan what exercise and when you're going to do it for the next three days. Put it in your calendar. This will get you thinking about planning your life around your exercise and happiness, rather than trying to fit it in around your already busy life.

When I've set this challenge for myself, my schedule usually looks something like this: Friday: weights 4–5 p.m., Saturday: cardio 11–12 p.m., Sunday: walk outside 3–4 p.m. For the next three days, make exercise your priority so you can feel happier. Are you in?

APRIL, Day 63: Drinking Culture in Sales

Having a fun drinking culture is not a mental health strategy. As offices open back up after the pandemic, it's going to be critical for sales teams to have a mental health strategy to support their reps.

I'm in full agreement that a fun drinking culture is a great part of working in sales. Some of the best friendships I have were formed through after-work drinks and team celebrations. But it can't be the only option, especially because it excludes salespeople who don't drink alcohol. New sales reps and new hires are highly impressionable. They want to fit in as quickly as possible because fitting in creates relationships that provide safety and comfort. As a result, new reps and hires look to follow the actions and behaviors of leaders or top performers. If that means joining managers for drinks at lunch or accompanying the #1 rep to a bar for drinks in the middle of the week, then that's what most will do.

Sales organizations need to take responsibility, and they need to create healthier opportunities for salespeople to develop bonds with teammates. More importantly, they need to educate them on how drinking affects their mental health, which then affects their sales performance. Providing healthier team-building options leads to healthier salespeople and healthier sales pipelines.

APRIL, Day 64: Prioritize Mental Health

I guarantee answering these two questions, which were shared by Tom Short on the *Live Better, Sell Better* podcast,[3] will help anyone better understand the importance of mental health in sales.

Question #1: Of all of the mistakes and/or errors that a typical salesperson or sales leader makes in performance, what percentage of them are "mental mistakes"?

A mental mistake is an error made in sales due to things like lack of confidence, composure, focus, or the inability to manage stress. For example, not feeling confident enough to ask a buyer a tough question during a sales pitch, or forgetting an important client detail because you're experiencing brain fog after a poor sleep the night prior. In my experience, most sellers and leaders I've spoken with agree that 80–100% of the mistakes they make on a daily basis are classified as mental mistakes.

Question #2: Of all of the training that is provided by a sales organization to their team, what percentage is spent on "mental training"?

Mental training involves training and coaching on topics, mindset, resilience, and mental health that help protect the brain from stress and reduce the frequency of mental mistakes that are made. From the hundreds of presentations I've delivered to sales organizations, when I ask this question to the audience, the range is usually between 0 and 5%.

By answering these two questions, it should be pretty clear that many sales organizations have a massive blind spot in how they think about mental health training in the context of sales performance. It should now be clear that sales is a performance-driven sport and investing into ways to reduce the frequency of mental mistakes being made is a guaranteed way to generate a massive ROI at the individual and team level.

APRIL, Day 65: Collaboration in Sales

As a result of remote working, many sales teams are trying to replace the loss of connection they're feeling with virtual team events and happy hours. A more effective solution is doubling down on collaboration.

Collaboration is defined as a group of two or more people working together to achieve a goal or find a creative solution to a tough problem together. This process of collaboration fosters deep connection between members in the group as they achieve something meaningful together. You might think that sales teams have targets and goals, so won't that lead to team collaboration and connection?

Unfortunately not and we can use the 2022 LA Lakers as an example to illustrate how *individual* sales targets prevent collaboration. Before a basketball game, if the head coach said:

"Lebron James, you need to score 25 points."
"Anthony Davis, you need to score 20 points."
"Russel Westbrook, you need to score 18 points."

And the coach then told each player if they missed their target, that individual would be traded to a new team, do you think that team would collaborate? If the game was on the line and one of those players was behind target, do you think they would make the individual sacrifices that were required to help the team win? Definitely not.

Sales organizations have long believed that the best way to increase performance is to get a group of salespeople to compete against each other, however here is what gets lost in a hyper-competitive environment:

- True peer-to-peer mentorship;
- Ability to leverage individual strengths;
- A united team vision and value set;
- Cooperation, collaboration, and connection;
- Authentic relationships;
- Environments supportive of mental health.

If sales organizations are expecting to perform in a hybrid working environment going forward, then it's time to start thinking about retiring individual targets and start experimenting with a team-based model where reps and managers can feel connected through one shared sales target. If considering this idea makes you uncomfortable as a leader, then some good questions to ask yourself are: Why do you fear giving up control? Why don't you trust your team to work together? Why do you think you need individual targets to hold people accountable? The answers to those questions are the real problems you need to focus on addressing first.

APRIL, Day 66: Sales Training Confusion

"Mental health training" is "sales training," and too many sales leaders I speak with think these trainings are different. They are not, and both can be classified as sales training that will help a sales team perform better and close more deals. In fact, investing into any kind of training that supports the mind and helps protect it from stressors in sales will compound the impact of all of the "traditional" sales training you're already investing thousands into.

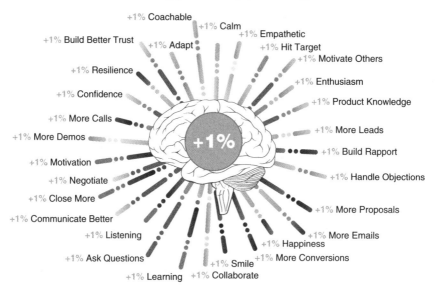

If you improve the health of the mind by 1%, you're going to be improving every other trait, skill, and aspect you consider to be important in sales. This is called exponential thinking and is the reason why data is showing that investment into areas related to mental health can improve the health and productivity of teams by a factor of three or even four.

Sales leaders need to stop thinking small, stop thinking this requires a different budget, and need to stop overcomplicating it. Mental health training *is* sales training, and all you need to do is use the budget you already have.

APRIL, Day 67: Lark or Owl?

Are you a lark or an owl? It's an important question that Matthew Walker brings up in his book *Why We Sleep* and one we should answer because aligning your natural sleep cycle to your workday can be one of the best ways to maximize your performance and improve mental health.[4]

According to Walker's research, 40% of people are "larks," who wake up early and go to bed early. Then 30% of people are "owls," who wake up late and go to bed late. And finally, 30% of people are somewhere in between.

Walker goes on to explain that one of the biggest failures in our workplaces is failing to acknowledge the different sleep needs of our employees. When we force workers into a nine-to-five routine, organizations could be hampering the performance of a large portion of their workforce due to poor sleep. Especially within sales, this will have a direct impact on productivity and motivation to keep selling. Larks can fade and tire before the end of the day, while owls can be groggy and half asleep in the morning.

I would encourage sales leaders to provide more flexibility to their sales teams around working hours to ensure they are maximizing their team's ability to sleep and recover from stress each night. Consider allowing larks to start work and end work one to two hours earlier, and allow owls to start work and end work one to two hours later. At the very least, this is something all leaders should experiment with for a month or two to see what happens to sales performance.

APRIL, Day 68: Have or Have Not

Prioritizing the well-being and mental health of salespeople is rapidly evolving. Several clients I've worked with over the last few years have created dedicated internal committees that are focused entirely on supporting sales teams' well-being. These committees are separate from HR, have decision-making power, and have access to budgets. This means mental health stigma in sales is breaking. Having vulnerable and supportive conversations is trending toward becoming the norm. Investment into the mental health space is also exploding.

A recent Crunchbase article from 2020 showed investors pumped almost $1 billion into companies focused on providing mental health services.[5] Why? Because there is a severe shortage of companies, therapists, and experts who are available to support the demand for more mental health services created by the fallout of the pandemic. As a result, there is a great divide growing between two types of companies, the "haves" and the "have nots."

The "haves" are companies that invested early, built internal infrastructure, and have support for their sales teams, while the "have nots" are companies that waited and are now experiencing poor sales performance and retention issues created by burnout. The HR department cannot be the only function focused on moving an organization into the haves column. Sales leaders need to play an active role in mental health conversations and allocate budgets accordingly.

APRIL, Day 69: Getting Mental Health Wrong

Data shows 62% of missed workdays can be attributed to mental health conditions.[6] Global rates of depression and anxiety have also increased 15% to 20% in the last decade. To reverse this trend, we have to stop getting these three areas of workplace mental health wrong:

1. **Overreliance on external services:**

   According to the Kaiser Family Foundation, about 39% of employers updated their health plans to include mental health services at the start of COVID.[7] Services include access to virtual therapy, which has proven to be an amazing resource that generates real results. However, this strategy still takes a "not my problem" approach by the company. Companies, and sales teams specifically, need to consider hiring a therapist or social worker internally who can provide ongoing resilience, mental health, and stress-management support to their teams.

2. **Overgeneralizing:**

   HR teams need to stop treating their organization like a collective whole and instead treat it like a collection of individual departments that will each face their own mental health struggles and stressors. For example, the stressors a salesperson regularly faces are going to be different than the stressors a software developer or the stressors a project manager might face. Overgeneralizing is leading to a war chest of mental health solutions being purchased but never getting used because they aren't tailored to meet the needs of different roles.

3. **Forgetting the why and the how:**

   The average salesperson knows mental health is important in general, but very few know how important it is to daily performance. If that connection between mental health and performance is not explicitly clear, mental health will continue to be an afterthought. In order to break these bad habits, salespeople need to be shown why and how looking after their mental health will help them perform better and achieve meaningful goals such as earning more commission or getting promoted. Without this type of context, the desire individuals have to take better care of themselves won't be there.

APRIL, Day 70: Languishing

Are you languishing today? The popular *New York Times* article defines this term as the feeling we get when we're feeling somewhat joyless, purposeless, and aimless.[8] According to Adam Grant, "Languishing is when you don't have symptoms of mental illness, but you're also not the picture of someone who is thriving with your mental health either." More importantly, what can you do on days when you're languishing? Here is my six-step process that you can follow:

STEP 1: Set Your Vision
    One week, one month, and one year from now, ask yourself who do you want to *become* that would make you proud? Maybe it's a better salesperson, parent, partner, entrepreneur, marathon runner, or chef; who are you striving to become in the future?

STEP 2: Define Your Why
    Why is it important that you become this future person? What would happen if you fail to become that person in the future? Would you regret it? Who else in your life (friends, family, colleagues, etc.) would benefit from you becoming that future you? This is your motivation. Write these reasons down and create a visual cue so they're easy to come back to.

STEP 3: Pick an Action
    What is one small action or behavior you can take *right now* to start becoming that person? For example: Put your gym clothes on, buy a website domain, start reading that book on your night stand, or, call that lead you've been avoiding; whatever it is, write that action down.

STEP 4: Commit and Countdown from 10 Seconds
    Say out loud and with conviction: "No matter what happens in the next 10 seconds, I'm going to *do* the action I've written down in step three when I get to zero." By adding this countdown component, you will stimulate the release of a tiny bit of adrenaline and cortisol that will get your body moving. Then start counting yourself down from 10 seconds out loud.

STEP 5: Go

STEP 6: Repeat Steps 3 through 6

APRIL, Day 71: Emotional Experiences

Here is a quick mindset hack that will help you manage your emotions. Rather than saying, "I am X (emotion)," try saying, "I am experiencing X."

When we say things such as "I am angry," "I am sad," "I am anxious," or "I am bored," we become engulfed in the emotions we're feeling. Our emotions can feel permanent, suffocating, and overwhelming. In this state, we're more likely to judge ourselves or blame others for how we're feeling, which usually increases the intensity of the emotion that we're feeling.

Instead, create space between yourself and your emotions by saying, "I am experiencing anger," "I am experiencing sadness," "I am experiencing anxiety," or "I am experiencing boredom." Experiences, like emotions, have a beginning, middle, and end. They are temporary. When emotions are temporary, they become easier to accept, and it becomes easier to manage the ebbs and flows of what you're feeling each day.

The most challenging part of this exercise is labeling the type of emotions that you're experiencing, so make sure you use the emotions wheel in the article below to help you identify what you're feeling. Only when you can label your emotions accurately will you be able to accept them as temporary emotional experiences that will soon pass.

Scan to access the Emotions Wheel to help you better understand the different emotions you're experiencing.

APRIL, Day 72: Napping in Sales

If you're open to experimenting with new ways to speed up your learning retention, try building naps into your daily routine. It may provide you with a 20% learning advantage.

In Matthew Walker's book *Why We Sleep*, he discusses the important role sleep plays in retaining new information.[9] When we're learning something new, such as facts about a new product or service we're going to be selling, all of this information gets stored in a short-term storage site of the brain called the hippocampus. The problem with the hippocampus is it can only retain a limited amount of new information throughout the day before it gets full. When this happens it becomes harder to concentrate and memorize new things. But here is where a good nap can help.

Walker's research showed that when we nap or sleep, our brain moves new information from this short-term storage site to a long-term vault called the cortex. This process clears space in the hippocampus for new information to absorb after the nap, while making it easier to remember the information we already learned. When comparing nappers and non-nappers in a study, nappers experienced a 20% learning advantage compared to those who skipped their afternoon siesta. A good reminder of the benefits that come with slowing down, in order to speed up in sales.

APRIL, Day 73: 20 Extra Days

If you're working for a company that supports remote working, then you recently gained an extra 20 days (roughly) a year to offload stress and improve yourself. When you think about it, in a pre-COVID world where working at the office was the norm, most people were commuting about two hours a day. Assuming two weeks' vacation a year, statutory holidays, and taking into account miscellaneous time away from work, no longer having to commute means you've gained an extra 10 hours a week. That's 480 hours a year, or an extra 20 days you previously spent on a bus, train, or sitting in traffic.

Maximizing this extra time will set you apart from the vast majority of people who will waste it. You need to be intentional with using the one hour you gained at the start of the day to prepare your brain for the day ahead and then using the hour at the end of the day to recover from the stressors you encountered throughout the day. Sticking to a daily routine like this prevents large swings in mood and mental health, which in turn will prevent large swings in motivation and sales performance. Don't fall into the trap of using this extra time to work more or waste it scrolling on your phone.

To the companies trying to force salespeople and leaders who previously commuted back into the office, this is why they're leaving. They aren't trading 20 days of free time for the same pay, same title, and same work environment. Nor should they have to.

APRIL, Day 74: Don't Be a Homer

Sales leaders need to stop setting sales targets like Homer Simpson. I will never forget watching Homer dancing around on the *Simpsons* many years ago singing: "I am so smart! . . . S . . . M . . . R . . . T . . ." after he started a fire in his own house. What a complete fool, I thought. No one would respect a person like that in real life. And the truth is they don't.

Most sales leaders today are setting "SMRT" sales targets but need to start setting "SMART" sales targets instead.

S - Specific

M - Measurable

A - Achievable

R - Relevant

T - Time-specific

If they leave out the "A" and make sales targets unachievable, their sales team will struggle with challenging emotions including anger and hopelessness, which affects their mental health, and they will lose the motivation they need to perform at a high level. Like Homer, these sales leaders will literally be burning the house their sales team works in, to the ground.

Do you really want to burn your sales culture to the ground? No. Do you really want to be the Homer Simpson of sales? No. So get SMART about it. Don't be a Homer.

Any sales leader can determine the achievability of a sales target by using the conversion rates at each stage of their sales pipeline. Is it humanly possible for a sales rep to execute the top-of-funnel volume metrics (calls, emails, etc.) required to generate enough demos, which generate enough proposals, which generate enough closed deals to hit the target within the month or quarter? If the answer is no, then someone is being a Homer. Don't forget to factor in vacation that sales reps have booked off ahead of time. They shouldn't be punished with an unachievable target and smaller commission check for taking well-deserved holidays.

APRIL, Day 75: Take a Mental Health Day

Don't be afraid to take a mental health day today if you need one. It's important to remember that we can all still experience burnout while working from home. Some may argue it's even more possible now than it was before remote working became popular. Uncertainty and times of rapid change are creating much higher levels of work and personal stress in a totally new environment.

Sales leaders, remind your team that it's okay to take a mental health day so self-care activities can be prioritized if your salespeople are starting to experience burnout. It might even be a good idea to discuss the symptoms of burnout as a team so everyone can look out for each other.

Typically, when I take a mental health day, my day is filled with meditations, alternating cold and hot showers, stretching, exercise, reading, board games, and a social media detox. If your stress levels are *really* high and you don't know what to do, consider speaking to your HR department to see what kind of mental health services you have access to. Most companies today have invested into virtual mental health services, which make it easy to talk to a trained professional from the comfort of your own home.

APRIL, Day 76: Control What You Can Control

When you work in sales it's very easy to feel like you have very little control over your job and your environment. Everything from how targets are set, your daily KPIs, when you get promoted, and when a deal closes is usually decided by someone else. A recent McKinsey article did an excellent job highlighting research on how important job control is to employee well-being and mental health: "Employees with more job control were healthier, absent from work less frequently and experienced less depression."[10]

Each day we all have a limited amount of energy. Far too often we spend this energy reacting to things in our environment we cannot control. You can't control if the person you are calling is in a bad mood or if your manager is anxious and micromanaging today. You can, however, control your mindset, which is made up of your beliefs, attitudes, and opinions toward these events. Pausing to adjust your attitude or reframe certain beliefs can help you perceive these uncontrollable events in a more positive light. You can also control your behavior and how you respond to these events. You can choose actions that create an upward spiral instead of a downward spiral when you're intentional with how you behave.

Be mindful of where you invest energy today, and make sure it's being used on things you *can* control. At the end of the day, reflect on how you did by making two lists: one list about what you could control and one list about what you could not control about what happened during the day. With practice you'll get better at accepting and letting go of the people, events, and experiences you could not control.

APRIL, Day 77: Get Involved

If you're a sales leader, you need to get involved with the mental health conversation because it affects every single person on your sales team.

Mental health is defined as a spectrum of well-being that we fluctuate along in response to changes in our internal environment (thoughts, feelings, emotions, etc.) and changes to our external environment (people we interact with, workplace, home, etc.). Similar to the physical health spectrum where people can be fit, healthy, overweight, obese, etc., every single person reading this page is functioning at some point on the mental health spectrum. Common words to describe where you fall on this mental health spectrum are the following: flourishing, healthy, coping, languishing, struggling, and unwell (dealing with a mental illness). Mental illness includes terms such as "anxiety," "depression," "burnout," "eating disorders," and "addiction" which are used when the *frequency*, *duration*, and *intensity* of declining mental health symptoms are all very high. For example, feeling a little anxious for a few days is way different than feeling highly anxious for multiple months and needing extended time off work.

Sales leaders run into challenges when they mistakenly interpret "mental health" as only applying to "mental illness." It would be equivalent to interpreting "physical health" as only applying to various "physical illnesses" such as high blood pressure, diabetes, or broken bones. As a result, leaders wait to support the mental health of their team and only jump in when they see sales reps who are struggling, hurt, or very unwell. This means there are days, weeks, months, or even years of underperformance leading up to this point. As salespeople move down the mental health spectrum (healthy → coping → struggling → unwell), daily sales performance suffers.

Recent data from the "2021 State of Mental Health in Sales Report" (mentioned on Day 56: Burnout and Control) shows that 58% of your sales team is likely falling into the "struggling" or "unwell" categories. Sales leaders, *you* need to play an active role in the mental health discussion if you desire peak performance from your team. This means providing mental health and resilience training that will help destigmatize this conversation and limit the impact external stressors (rejection, deals falling through, etc.) have on performance.

Peak performance is achieved when we can keep our sales teams mentally healthy and limit how much fluctuation happens along this mental health spectrum on a daily basis.

APRIL, Day 78: Protect Your Players

Would you send a football player onto the field without pads or a soldier into battle without armor or a shield? Probably not, so why are we treating salespeople like this?

"Sales is a contact sport" said every sales manager ever, and they're right. You are going to get hit by rejection *a lot* in sales. Usually multiple times a day you'll get knocked to the ground and have to pick yourself back up. This hurts, and it wears you down, especially if you don't know how to protect yourself. If you don't know how to navigate stressors and recover from stress properly, these injuries linger and follow you home. They affect relationships and influence the development of bad habits or addictions to help us escape from the emotional pain we're feeling.

This is why I believe every organization has a responsibility to give their salespeople pads and shields before they play and do battle. Training and coaching that a company has built into every onboarding process will help salespeople protect their mental health. It's the company's game, battle, product, and environment. Salespeople are there to help the company win, so management must ensure they are not using them as cannon fodder and protect them.

With that in mind, Mental Health Awareness month is coming up in May. What do you have planned for your sales team?

APRIL, Day 79: Your To-Do List

How many tasks on your to-do list would be categorized as self-care, recovery, or other activities that support your mental health? The answer I normally hear is zero. Your to-do list will usually paint a perfect picture of your daily priorities and provide immediate answers to why you're feeling burnt out and overwhelmed.

When you plan 100% of your time each day to focus on working and serving others, it's no wonder there is no time for the most important person in your life—*you*. If we don't plan activities that support showing up as our best self each day, these activities will be the first things that we cut or forget to do when we're working under a deadline. As our mental health declines—so will our performance.

For the next seven working days I challenge you to add three tasks to your to-do list each day that are entirely focused on recovery and helping you lower your stress levels. By simply thinking about these activities ahead of time and planning them into your day, my bet is you'll do a much better job prioritizing what *you* need, to do your best work and be your best self each day.

APRIL, Day 80: Proactive Sales Onboarding

Do you currently hire a lot of fresh college graduates or people new to sales? If so, it's naïve to think that someone who is new to sales has the toolkit they need to minimize stress and maximize the mental components required to perform in sales.

Unfortunately, our current education system and society are still doing a relatively poor job equipping younger generations with stress-management strategies before entering the workforce. This means the responsibility is falling on companies and sales organizations to support them.

A great place to start providing mental health and resilience training is during new sales hire onboarding because it's a *proactive strategy* any sales team can use to support better mental health and sales performance. These programs also integrate seamlessly into the new hire experience in the following ways:

1. New sales hires are already in the *"training mindset"* and likely expecting some virtual learning.
2. There is no pressure from targets or quota, which means learning and retention will be maximized.
3. It's an opportunity to reinforce a more supportive sales culture and reduce mental health stigma across the organization.
4. These programs also provide new hires with the tools they need to protect their mental health before they enter a high stress environment.

Mental health and resilience training is also a perk job seekers would be excited to hear about. When I polled my network with the following question "How would you feel if a company provided sales-specific mental health and resilience training during new hire onboarding?" 6% of salespeople said they would be less excited to work for the company, 17% would feel about the same and 77% said they would be more excited to work for the company.

We have to remember that anxiety in sales is *not* optional. It's part of everyday life. Sales organizations that are taking a proactive approach to mental health are going to flourish as it continues to be a growing interest and topic of concern for future generations.

APRIL Endnotes

1. Hussain, Y. "Posthaste: Canadians are financially stressed but would switch to a lower paying job in a heartbeat for this one perk." *Financial Post.* January 28, 2020. https://financialpost.com/executive/posthaste-canadians-are-financially-stressed-but-they-will-switch-to-a-lower-paying-job-in-a-heartbeat-for-this-one-perk.

2. Moynihan, R. "Exercise makes you happier than having money, according to Yale and Oxford research." World Economic Forum. April 9, 2019. https://www.weforum.org/agenda/2019/04/exercise-officially-makes-you-happier-than-money-according-to-yale-and-oxford-research.

3. Dorsey, K. "Mind Is Everything with Tom Short." *Live Better, Sell Better* Podcast. June 22, 2020. https://live-better-sell-better.simplecast.com/episodes/mindset-is-everything-with-tom-short-a2Aw9VYU.

4. Walker, M. *Why We Sleep*. Penguin Books, 2018.

5. Hall, C. "Access To Mental Health: Startups Tackle Sector's Complexities As Investors Go All-in." Crunchbase News. February 22, 2021. https://news.crunchbase.com/health-wellness-biotech/access-to-mental-health-startups-tackle-sectors-complexities-as-investors-go-all-in/.

6. Vasilev, E. "The Financial Cost Of Ignoring Mental Health In The Workplace." Forbes Finance Council. January 8, 2020. https://www.forbes.com/sites/forbesfinancecouncil/2020/01/08/the-financial-cost-of-ignoring-mental-health-in-the-workplace/?sh=1ded8a785e92.

7. "2021 Employer Health Benefits Survey." Kaiser Family Foundation. 2021. https://www.kff.org/health-costs/report/2021-employer-health-benefits-survey/.

8. Grant, A. "There's a Name for the Blah You're Feeling: It's Called Languishing." *New York Times*. April 19, 2021. https://www.nytimes.com/2021/04/19/well/mind/covid-mental-health-languishing.html.

9. Walker, M. *Why We Sleep*. Penguin Books, 2018.

10. Pfeffer, J. "The overlooked essentials of employee well-being." McKinsey Quarterly. September 11, 2018. The overlooked essentials of employee well-being | McKinsey.

MAY

MAY, Day 81: Say NO More

"No" is a powerful word that will help you improve your mental health while working in sales. My girlfriend reminded me of the importance of saying no when making decisions each day. Saying yes to opening one door means you're saying no to opening a different door, and there is always a trade-off.

Saying yes to overworking while working from home means you're saying no to spending more time with your family and a good night's rest. Saying yes to a client request you know your team can't deliver in order to close the sale means saying no to setting proper expectations with the client and managing your team's workload effectively. Saying yes to sending your colleagues an email or Slack message after hours means saying no to setting proper boundaries for yourself.

We live in a sales culture that makes us constantly feel like we have to fit in and people-please. We feel like we have to always say yes for other people to like us. Whether it's with the buyers we speak with on a daily basis or relentlessly seeking the approval of our manager, saying yes makes it easy to lose sight of who we are. We become obsessed with chasing who others want us to be; it's exhausting.

In this world we burn out. There is no room for what we *want* and what we *need*, and it becomes impossible to be our authentic selves. The more depleted our wants and needs become, the less resilient we become to stress. When this happens our sales performance and mental health decline.

Setting strong boundaries and saying no to things that others believe you should say yes to makes you vulnerable to their judgments. But within these vulnerable moments you also show strength. In a world of *yes people*, the word "no" stands out. Saying no allows you to protect your needs and wants so you can remain authentic to yourself and genuine to others. These are characteristics that your colleagues, managers, and buyers will respect and admire.

Over the next few days, be mindful of what you're saying yes to. Ask yourself, "Is this what I really want or need right now?" Make sure saying yes doesn't mean saying no to the things that truly make you happy and help you recover from a stressful day on the sales floor.

MAY, Day 82: Recovery Metrics

Until sales teams start tracking recovery metrics, sales performance and burnout will always be a problem. We are *not* built to sell all the time without proper rest and recovery periods built into our day. This is why I have been using a product called WHOOP, which is essentially a FitBit on steroids, to manage my recovery and maximize my performance on a daily basis.

One of the most important metrics WHOOP provides is a daily "Recovery Score." This number tells you how well-recovered and rested your body is. It also determines how much strain (aka stress) your body is prepared to take on both physically and mentally that day. WHOOP calculates your Recovery Score using an algorithm that measures changes to your HRV (heart rate variability), respiratory rate, resting heart rate, and how well you've slept. For example, decreases in your respiratory rate and heart rate indicate your body is under lower levels of stress and well rested.

One of the keys to managing burnout in sales is learning how to add and offload stress in equal parts each day. This has become much easier using the data WHOOP provides to help me make micro-changes each day to maximize recovery periods and daily performance. At a team level, there is also a really exciting company called LEON Health Science, which is making a big splash in this space, with predictive analytics to help sales managers better understand and adjust to their team's stress levels. I highly recommend checking out both when you have a free moment today.

MAY, Day 83: Personal Growth

When we *expect* business growth from people, our sales teams burn out. Expecting business growth from people conditions us to believe that good growth means performance should *always* be moving up and to the right. Any deviation from this "perfect" curve indicates a "problem," but this is simply not true.

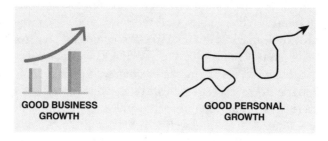

Image Source: Flaticon.com

Our sales teams consist of people, *not* machines. People learn best when they are in a safe environment to try new things, make mistakes, and fail forward. Personal growth is messy and nonlinear. When leaders stop expecting good business growth from people and aim for good personal growth instead, they immediately change their perspective on what high performance actually looks like. They become more compassionate to their people. They accept steps back and steps down as part of the process. They stop trying to jam a square peg into a circular hole and focus on building environments where *humans* can thrive, not machines.

If you're a sales leader, as you look at your dashboard today, if you see a rep investing the effort, practice, and learning to get better each day, but they just suffered a major setback, remind them that's part of the process. It is what personal growth feels like. Let them know it's okay.

MAY, Day 84: Unlimited PTO Is Not Enough

There appears to be one common objection most forward-thinking organizations use when I approach them about a mental health solution: "We provide unlimited time off and mental health days—we're good."

While I applaud organizations for allowing their employees to take time off when they need it, they're missing the point when they lean too heavily on require off. This is a *reactive* strategy. When salespeople absolutely need time off or take a mental health day, the damage from stress and declining mental health has likely already been done. It's like an athlete who keeps getting injured and is not given the training to prevent the injury in the future. Sure, you could argue that's what employee benefits are for, but how many salespeople actually use these benefits in a *preventative* way?

Sales is a mental game, and an effective mental health strategy helps your team become more resilient by teaching them how to use stress to their advantage so they can learn how to respond to stressors such as missing targets, and daily rejection that can often affect performance for days or weeks before a manager might notice. This is especially important when reps are working from home or remotely. A preventative strategy like adding a mandatory time-off component to unlimited PTO policies will keep your players on the field so they can score.

MAY, Day 85: Climb Down into the Hole

I've had a few sales leaders tell me that PIPs (performance improvement programs) are a good motivation tool. I agree, but only when they are framed and used as a way to genuinely help the rep like we discussed on Day 03: PIP 2.0. However, in my experience they are often framed and used in the wrong way. They are framed as a whip and used as a way to motivate a sales rep through fear of losing their job. This is inhumane. It also rarely works. Even if it generates the short-term results a sales leader may be looking for, the long-term effect it has on the rep and their negative perception of the company is never worth it.

Instead, when the same performance issue keeps arising, sales leaders need to be brave and dig deeper into understanding why the rep is actually underperforming. They need to show compassion, be vulnerable themselves, and be willing to climb down into the hole their rep is stuck in. The sales rep is likely scared, experiencing burnout, struggling with their mental health, and lost in a sea of emotion. They need the leader's help, and they need to trust the leader before they can open up.

When sales leaders look down on reps trapped in the hole and add more fear to their lives using a performance improvement program, the sales rep sinks even deeper. Sales leaders need to learn how to meet them in the darkness, and if they don't know how, then there is a gap in leadership training that needs to be filled immediately.

If you need help having more vulnerable conversations with your team, then scan here to view the Sales Leader Fundamentals program I deliver to leadership teams to help them navigate difficult conversations in sales and build trust with their team.

MAY, Day 86: Mental Health Cost Calculator

Do you know how much mental health is costing your team specifically in sales performance? Now you can find out with the Sales Mental Health Cost Calculator that I built with my good friend Jason Chen.

When we think about mental health costs within sales, the majority of these costs are due to presenteeism and absenteeism. Presenteeism happens when sales reps show up to work and their mental health is in a suboptimal state which results in lost productivity. Absenteeism happens when their mental health has declined to a point when they can't show up at all. Presenteeism, specifically, is much harder to track and the lost productivity is felt when sales reps engage in low-performance activities such as making fake dials to hit metrics and praying for voicemails, or when they make mistakes, miss buying signals, have less empathy, sell without confidence, avoid objections, ask easy questions, and/or avoid the decision maker.

When sales teams become anxious, depressed, or burnt out, their sales performance suffers. Now with the calculator below you can find out exactly what that looks from a sales perspective and find answers on:

- How many calls are you or your team missing?
- How many meetings are you or your team missing?
- How much closed revenue are you or your team missing?
- How much is salary costing the company?

Sample calculation of a 20-person sales team using the calculator:

How much is mental health costing your sales team?

Sales Health Alliance

Answer these Questions:	Input Your Answer Here	Units
How many salespeople are you responsible for?	20	Staff
On average how many calls does each rep make?	50	/Day
On average how many meetings does each rep book?	2	/Day
What is the average base salary of your reps?	$50,000	/Year
On average how much revenue does each rep close?	$15,000	/Month
Number of working/selling days per year	220	/Year

Calculations based on the following:	Locked Fields (Do Not Change)	Units
Prevalance Rate: 58% of salespeople struggle with their Mental Health	58.00%	Percent
Average absenteeism: Sick days due to mental health per year	7.5	/Year
Average presenteeism: Lost productivity days due to mental health per year	8	/Year
Average Absenteeism & Presenteeism likely much higher in sales		

Sales Mental Health Costs Per Year	Your Mental Health Costs	Units
How many potential calls that do not get made.	8,990	/Year
How many potential meeting that do not get booked.	360	/Year
How much potential revenue that does not get closed.	$147,109	/Year
Salary costs due to unproductive and missed days.	$40,864	/Year
Total Mental Health Costs (Lost Revenue + Salary Costs)	**$187,973**	/Year

Calculated based off 58% of your salespeople struggling with their Mental Health and each losing 15.5 selling days per year.

Are you brave enough to see the answers to these questions? The impact will definitely surprise you. If you're a sales leader, next time you're evaluating a flashy new sales enablement technology that is claiming to make your team more efficient, pause and ask yourself: Will it address all the low performance activities above, or should I start prioritizing mental health solutions instead?

 Scan here to download and access the Sales Mental Health Cost Calculator to see the hidden costs in your own team.

MAY, Day 87: Uncle Ben

Uncle Ben said it best when he told Peter Parker, "With great power comes great responsibility." For everyone reading this, your power comes in the form of your prefrontal cortex (PFC), and it's the greatest gift you have. It also requires tremendous responsibility to wield this power effectively.

Our brain weighs roughly 3% of our body mass, but it uses 20% of our energy. The PFC sits at the front of the brain, and humans have the largest one in the animal kingdom. This area of the brain is responsible for executive brain functions such as learning, impulse control, focus, problem solving, creativity, and imagination. It's how humans have become the dominant species in the world, and this part of our brain needs to be online if we hope to achieve our goals, manage our emotions, and feel motivated each day.

The problem is the PFC is very fragile because the brain uses an extremely lean operating system and all areas of the brain can't be operating at 100% capacity all of the time. There is an energy budget, which gets shared across all brain regions. When we are unable to cope with a stressor or we're experiencing chronic stress, other parts of our brain start demanding more energy, which robs our PFC and forces it to power down. In turn, we not only lose our most valuable coping tool but we lose the tool we need to thrive and be successful.

So today remember Uncle Ben's wise words: "With great power comes great responsibility." You have a great power inside of you, and it's your responsibility to protect it. Become a superhero by managing your stress throughout the day effectively so you can put your superpower to good use each and every day.

MAY, Day 88: Stop and Check

"I'd always end up broken down on the highway. When I stood there trying to flag someone down nobody stopped. But when I pushed my own car, other drivers would get out and push with me. If you want help, help yourself—people like to see that."

—**Chris Rock**

When I was a full-time salesperson, this quote resonated with me after a tough month on the sales floor, where it felt like I just couldn't catch a break. When I was a sales leader, it felt even more true. I was drawn to helping the people on my team who were putting the time and effort in every day to try and get better regardless of outcomes.

But when it comes to mental health, it feels less true. There are going to be days when we break down—days when anxiety, depression, and burnout will paralyze us. As much as we want to get out of the car and start pushing, we can't seem to find the energy or strength to do so. Even worse, society and our peers can make us feel guilty or become judgmental. Like there is something wrong with us if we break down.

As a teammate we have to remember that if someone isn't pushing their car and putting in the effort one day, it doesn't mean they're lazy or don't care. They may just need some help and are too afraid to ask. It's always best to stop and check.

MAY, Day 89: The Wim Hof Method

I've been meditating consistently for about eight years now, and one meditation technique stands out among everything I've tried. It's called the Wim Hof Method and was created by Wim Hof, aka the "Iceman." The practice uses a combination of deep breathing and cold therapy to help reactivate our body's natural ability to become more resilient.

In recent years humans have become obsessed with comfort, and in doing so, we have dulled two key systems in the body that help us respond to physical and mental stress: the autonomic nervous system and immune system. Both of these systems have long been viewed as scientifically impossible to control; however, recent studies done on the Wim Hof Method have shown they can indeed be voluntarily controlled through the practice. Benefits are varied and range from increased energy to stronger immune systems to reduced stress levels.[1]

Before learning this method, I would regularly struggle with anxiety, insomnia, and migraines. In all cases, the Wim Hof Method has played a critical role in reducing the severity of them or even stopping them entirely when they arose. It takes practice to build a new behavior like this into a habit, but I consistently use this method several times a week and have never felt better than I do today.

MAY, Day 90: The Power of "Yet"

Five letters have the potential to shut down our growth, lower our self-esteem, and make us feel like a failure in sales: "I can't." We unconsciously say it hundreds of times a day without even noticing it.

- "I can't cold-call."
- "I can't reach my prospect."
- "I can't get a job."
- "I can't hit my target."
- "I can't speak in public."
- "I can't find product-market fit."
- "I can't find love."
- "I can't dance."
- "I can't cook."
- "I can't afford a house."

The worst part about "I can't" and why it can affect us so heavily is because it can feel permanent. It can feel like we were born with a genetic flaw or living within an environment that keeps us from achieving certain goals or acquiring skills we need to live a meaningful life. When we accept "I can't" into our belief system, we usually give up, quit, and retreat into our comfort zone. It's the epitome of having a fixed mindset. The best part is you can change your mindset with three letters: "Yet."

- "I can't cold-call . . . yet."
- "I can't reach my prospect . . . yet."
- "I can't get a job . . . yet."
- "I can't hit my target . . . yet."
- "I can't speak in public . . . yet."
- "I can't find product-market fit . . . yet."
- "I can't find love . . . yet."
- "I can't dance . . . yet."
- "I can't cook . . . yet."
- "I can't afford a house . . . yet."

Injecting "yet" into your thought pattern fosters hope and compassion that allows you to accept that these skills and goals are not permanent states you have to live with. They're temporary. With a commitment to patience, discipline, hard work, and learning, we can change ourselves and change our undesirable situation over time. It's the epitome of a growth mindset.

So what are you working toward that you can't do . . . yet?

MAY, Day 91: Visualizing Sleep

Trying to sleep when you're worried about a sales target or stressed out from work can be a struggle. I've been experimenting with a new way to fall asleep that has been extremely effective, but I hadn't heard about it before: visualizing yourself sleeping.

The benefits of visualization have long been studied and can improve many areas of your life such as building confidence, learning a new skill, reducing stress, and achieving your goals. With sleep I've always read about visualization being used to do things such as "visualize yourself laying on a beach, swinging in a hammock, or floating on a raft in the water." This has never worked for me, because the sensations were too far removed from what it felt like to lie in my own bed. Instead, I've been experiencing success falling asleep quickly by doing the following:

I close my eyes and visualize watching myself yawn three to five times, as if I'm watching myself sleep from the perspective of a fly.

From this perspective, I visualize myself lying in the exact position I'm currently lying in, so the physical sensations match what I'm visualizing in my head.

Then I visualize myself drifting off to sleep.

Finally, I visualize myself sleeping and focus on how comfortable and relaxed I look asleep.

If you've been having trouble sleeping recently, give it a try because it's a visualization technique that tends to knock me out extremely quickly.

MAY, Day 92: Where Is the Off-Ramp?

I'm pretty sure 99.9% of the sales world is using the phrase "Reps are on-ramp" incorrectly when they talk about new hires ramping up.

Think about what an "on-ramp" actually is. It's a period of *buildup* while entering the highway, followed by a period of *intensity* while driving on the highway, followed by a period of *slowing down* when exiting the highway. If we forget the slowing down part, and we never allow our reps to get off the highway, then it's just *burnout*.

We can't keep our cars and we can't keep our people on the highway for an indefinite amount of time, because how long do you think that car or sales reps will go before it runs out of gas or breaks down? Not very far and will likely require some expensive repairs over the long term.

MAY, Day 93: Toxic Sales Dashboards

Most sales leaderboards are perpetuating a toxic culture of "What have you done for me lately?" This often makes sales reps anxious and can create a state of fear, which shuts down their logical brain and prevents them from performing at their best in sales.

Competition between individual reps is important to a certain degree, but leaderboards are missing one key component: competition with yourself. This requires historical performance data to be visible so reps and managers can focus on personal growth, rather than constantly comparing themselves to each other in the current month or quarter. Here are some individual growth metrics to consider:

1. Lifetime revenue closed;
2. All-time best month/quarter/year in revenue;
3. Most dials and meetings booked in a day;
4. Fastest deal closed;
5. Best streak and running streak of meeting daily KPIs in a row;
6. Best streak and current streak of consecutive months/quarters achieving target;
7. Biggest deal closed;
8. Total "Assists of the Day" or times the individual has helped others;
9. Total referrals;
10. Total testimonials collected.

These metrics will help individual reps be more compassionate to themselves on tough days, while helping sales leaders develop a better appreciation for their reps' growth, work, and total contributions to the company over time. What personal growth metrics would you like to see on your dashboard?

MAY, Day 94: Sharing Openly

As part of Mental Health Awareness month you may be thinking about sharing your story and experience with mental health with others. Here is what I've learned from doing it regularly.

Opening up your inner world to others is an extremely vulnerable experience. Sharing your story will usually mean sharing your deepest insecurities and fears that you've spent years hiding. Your ego doesn't like this. Your ego thrives when it's hidden in the darkness of your mind as it works to protect what it perceives as "weakness" or "faults" from the judgment of others. Sharing your story means shining a spotlight on your ego and saying, "I see you. I accept you. And this is me." You'll feel totally exposed but also totally free at the same time. Some people may judge you, but way more people will champion your authenticity. You'll connect with friends, family, and colleagues on a much deeper level than ever before by sharing the real you.

Like learning a new skill, being vulnerable takes practice. I'd recommend starting small and opening up to the people close to you first. Always approach your inner struggle from a place of growth, learning, and gratitude in how it has shaped you into the person you are today. Sharing this learning and growth will help others overcome their own struggles and normalize these types of conversations with the people closest to you.

MAY, Day 95: Why Are You Angry?

Are you feeling angry today? Anger can become overwhelming when we can't label why we are angry, so here are two questions to help you label the source of your anger.

1. Why do you feel unsafe?

Anger is an extremely powerful emotion that allows the body to take strong, powerful actions to defend itself from danger. It's the *fight* part of our fight-or-flight system. This system is programmed to use our memories and past experiences to scan our current environment for threats that may hurt us. Asking this question will help you identify why you feel unsafe or feel in danger. Try to determine what behaviors your partner, colleagues, or manager are taking that may be making you feel unsafe. Can you trace them back to a hurtful experience in the past that is clouding your judgment and causing you to misperceive their behavior as dangerous? (Example 1: Your current partner using their phone or social media may unintentionally make you feel unsafe and therefore angry because a previous partner cheated on you. Example 2: The way your current manager gives feedback may unintentionally remind you of a previous manager who bullied and fired you without notice.)

Once you can make this connection between behaviors in the present that trigger hurtful memories of the past, try sharing them with the person that is unintentionally making you feel unsafe with their actions. Most people will be happy to modify their behaviors once they're aware of why they make you upset.

2. What core values were crossed?

We all have a core value and belief system that governs our expectation of how people and the world should function. We want to protect these core values, and anger can provide fuel to protect our value system and fight for them. Do you know what your core values are? Here are some examples: justice, generosity, caring, cooperation, compassion, accountability, courage, and tradition. Mine are respect for others, honesty, and loyalty. When I get upset, I can usually trace the source of my anger back to an action someone has taken that I perceived as going against one of these core values. If I feel like all three are simultaneously crossed, then I tend to get really upset.

But again, have you shared your core values with the people around you? Have you shared how certain actions trigger your value system? If someone has a core value of being risk averse and their partner believes taking risks leads to opportunity, then it's very likely these two value systems will drive different expectations and behaviors that will create conflict. When we share our value systems with others, we can find ways to meet in the middle. This is how we co-create a shared set of expectations that help both parties feel valued and supported.

MAY, Day 96: Components of Hope

How do you stay motivated when no one is responding to your sales outreach? A great place to start is to foster more hope for yourself in sales.

When we're in a dark tunnel, hope is a powerful emotion that pushes us to keep going when we're feeling scared, lost, and uncertain. When we want to give up, it's that voice in our head telling us to keep going because it knows eventually we'll see the light at the end of the tunnel. It makes us gritty during tough months on the sales floor because we can envision the payoff for our struggle in the future. So if hope is so important, then how do we create more of it?

In her book *Dare to Lead*, Brené Brown talks about hope having three key components[2]: First, you need to have a *goal*. Second, you need to have a *path* to achieve that goal. Third, you need to have *agency*. In sales you have a goal in the form of a target and a path to get there in the form of a sales process. What most sales reps are missing is agency, which is the ability to have free will and make choices that will help them achieve their goal. Far too often sales processes are too rigid or structured, and as a result, they remove agency from the individual sales rep to problem-solve effectively. In doing so they snuff out hope, making it harder for reps to persevere.

Sales leaders, start thinking about how you can inject more free will and agency into your sales process so your team can feel more hopeful. Especially during challenging times, experimenting with a sales process that hasn't been modified in several months can make all the difference in solving the challenges your team is facing and keeping reps motivated.

MAY, Day 97: Not Feeling Motivated? Read This

Do you find yourself showing up to work not feeling motivated? You're not alone. Working in sales is exhausting, and most salespeople have an extremely difficult time motivating themselves on an ongoing basis.

This is worsened by the fact that most sales leaders don't understand motivation and therefore don't know how to help their team find it. When their team loses motivation, they opt for manipulative tactics instead of practical strategies that help. They use things such as fear, micromanagement, gamification, or other dopamine-driven incentives to get their team moving. When that external reward such as a target or incentive is achieved, what usually happens? Motivation plummets until the next carrot for the rep to chase is placed in front of them. This leads to inconsistent sales performance and makes working in sales feel less meaningful.

What individual salespeople and leaders are failing to understand is that motivation is essentially a state of arousal. When they're not motivated, they are likely either hypo-aroused or hyper-aroused. When salespeople are hypo-aroused, they're not *aroused enough*, alert, and lack the energy to complete the task at hand. Typically this happens after coming back from vacation or perhaps after a big lunch in the middle of the day. Alternatively, when salespeople are hyper-aroused, their arousal level is too high, and they feel so anxious that they start making mental mistakes or feel paralyzed and opt for procrastination instead. This tends to happen when salespeople have overworked themselves and neglected areas in their life that help them offload stress.

The first step in regaining your motivation is determining what *state* your mind and body is currently in. Are you more hypo-aroused or more hyper-aroused? Step two is choosing a strategy that helps you *raise your arousal level* when you're hypo-aroused or *lower your arousal level* when you're hyper-aroused.

I've outlined several strategies to adjust your arousal levels up or down in this article, so scan here to give them a read.

MAY, Day 98: Impact of Job Security

Feeling safe in our role and having job security is a key driver of psychological safety. One shocking new data point we uncovered with UNCrushed and The Harris Consulting Group in the "2021 Mental Health in Sales Survey" was that among salespeople who strongly agreed that they had job security and felt like their role was safe, 96% rated their sales performance as good or better. Within this group, 41% of salespeople rated their sales performance as excellent. Imagine how much less stressful your day-to-day would be as a leader if almost 100% of the reps on your team were performing well?

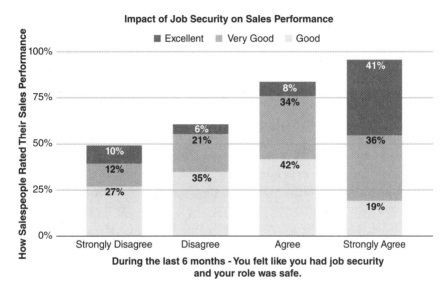

Image Source: T. Clarke, R. Harris, J. Riseley. "2021 State of Mental Health in Sales Report." UNCrushed, Sales Health Alliance, The Harris Consulting Group. May 2021. https://theharrisconsultinggroup.com/state-of-mental-health-in-sales-report.

Behind all of the anxiety, sleepless nights, arguments, and self-doubt that we experience in our daily lives, one foundational need is almost always never being met when we experience these symptoms of declining mental health: safety. We as humans need to feel safe. Providing more safety and security to a sales team (not less) is the first step in moving an individual from surviving in their environment to thriving in their environment.

MAY, Day 99: Being Supportive

It can be hard to know what to say and what to do when a colleague is feeling anxious and shares something vulnerable. Too often we can actually make things worse. Following this process has helped me offer better support in these situations:

Step 1 - Support: "I really appreciate you sharing this with me . . . I know that probably wasn't easy to get off your chest."

Step 2 - Relate: "When I'm feeling anxious or going through similar situations, I sometimes find it hard for other people to support me in the right way."

Step 3 - Clarify: "So help me get a better understanding of what you *need* right now. Do you need me to listen *or* do you need me to provide advice?"

Far too often when we see someone we care about struggling, our natural response is to try and make them feel better as quickly as possible. In sales, this happens all the time when managers fail to slow down and listen. They have a bad habit of quickly jumping into problem-solving mode and start offering up sales strategies or advice to try and remedy declining performance. This approach is backward, and before offering advice, managers first need to pause and clarify what their reps need most. Often when they're feeling anxious, they need a manager who is willing to listen and help them sort through the uncomfortable emotions they're feeling first. Problem solving and creating an action plan usually comes second.

MAY, Day 100: Choosing the Right Type of Meditation

Mindfulness meditation has exploded as a popular strategy to relieve stress and negative thinking, but you need to be careful how you use it. Understanding the nuances between *different types* of mindfulness meditation is important because in some situations choosing the wrong type can be negative.

This was discovered when research found that *breath-focused mindfulness meditation* can decrease feelings of guilt and other negative emotions. This sounds amazing, but not so fast. Are all negative emotions bad things we should avoid? Assistant Professor Andrew Hafenbrack at the University of Washington put things in perspective by sharing this viewpoint with PsyPost[3]: "Focused breathing mindfulness meditation reliably reduces negative emotions, which makes people feel better. However, all emotions are partly a form of information and in many cases when we ignore that information, we put ourselves in peril."

Guilt for example, provides important feedback that pushes people to make amends and repair important relationships they have with others. This was seen in a meta-analysis of 17,000 people, where researchers showed that dampening feelings of guilt through *mindfulness breathing meditation* also reduced kind and helping behavior.[4]

Sales and the modern workplace create environments that stir up uncomfortable emotions every single day. Mindfulness meditation can be a helpful tool you use to take care of your mental health, but the data above shows that choosing the right type of meditation is important. When you're dealing with the emotional sting created by a stranger you just cold-called or a deal you lost due to factors outside your control, by all means, dampen these emotions and lean into a meditation that focuses on *controlling your breath*. However, when you're dealing with the emotional sting created by an argument or conflict with a colleague, partner, or person you care about, try a *loving-kindness meditation* instead (different type of mindfulness meditation you can google or look up on your meditation app). Hafenbrack says this increases your focus on other people and increases positive emotions such as love that will help you resolve your conflict in a meaningful way, instead of calming down using your breath and avoiding it.

MAY Endnotes

1. "The Science Behind The Wim Hof Method." Wim Hof Method. https://www.wimhofmethod.com/science

2. Brown, B. *Dare to Lead: Brave Work. Tough Conversations. Whole Hearts.* Diversified Publishing, 2019.
3. Dolan, E. "Mindfulness meditation reduces prosocial reparative behaviors by buffering people against feelings of guilt." PsyPost. April 16, 2022. https://www.psypost.org/2022/04/mindfulness-meditation-reduces-prosocial-reparative-behaviors-by-buffering-people-against-feelings-of-guilt-62925.
4. Donald, J. N., Sahdra, B. K., Van Zanden, B., Duineveld, J. J., Atkins, P. W. B., Marshall, S. L., and Ciarrochi, J. (2019). "Does your mindfulness benefit others? A systematic review and meta-analysis of the link between mindfulness and prosocial behaviour." *British Journal of Psychology* (London, England: 1953), 110(1), 101–125. https://doi.org/10.1111/bjop.12338.

JUNE

JUNE, Day 101: Craft, Mind, and Body

The entire sales industry is playing checkers, when they should be playing chess because we're getting high performance wrong in sales right now. My friend Tom Short broke this down for me in the simplest way, which any sales leader or individual contributor should be able to understand.

Developing a high-performing team or individual in sports or sales requires simultaneously developing three key pillars:

1. Your craft;
2. Your mind;
3. Your body.

In my experience, 95% of sales organizations are investing 100% of their training budget and time into "craft." They're forgetting that sales is primarily a mental game, which requires equal investments of time and practice into improving the mind and body. If you want to be a top performer or top team, then mental health is not something you try to squeeze in if you have time. It's not something to be feared and swept under the rug. It's also not something you check off in hopes of avoiding a wrongful dismissal lawsuit. Prioritizing mental health is *the key* to high performance that everyone in sales is missing. It unlocks the door to becoming a pro.

JUNE, Day 102: Who Do You Want to Be?

As kids, we were all asked, "Who do you want to be when you grow up?" We need to keep asking it as adults because it ensures we're consistently working toward a future version of ourselves.

The reason this question is so powerful is because it asks children to think about who they want to *become* when they're older. It's about a future identity they want to achieve: "I want to be a fireman," "I want to be a doctor," "I want to be just like my mom." Too often this is perceived as just a silly question and a game we can play with our kids, but this question in the hands of an adult can be *powerful*. As we grow older, many of us change this question to focus on external rewards or material possessions: "What do we want to achieve in the future?" "I want a new house," "I want a new promotion," "I want to get married." It's as if we reach a point in our lives when we stop growing and stop thinking about who we want our future self to be.

We need to keep growth and our future identity in mind because it will help keep us accountable to taking better actions every single day. Stop asking yourself *what* you want and instead start asking yourself *who* you want to grow up to be this month, this year, and five years from now. What habits and choices would that future self start implementing today? Embedding these habits and choices into a daily routine is how you evolve into that person over time. It's a tough question to answer, but spend time journaling about it today: *Who do you want to be when you grow up, and what habits would they have?*

JUNE, Day 103: The NFL and Sales

"Not for long." Many joke that is what the NFL stands for, but this statement also rings true for many working in sales. Sales and football are high-contact sports, and both the sales industry and the NFL take a similar approach to how they treat their people and players. Rarely is any money guaranteed long term and prior individual successes can be quickly forgotten. If you're hurt physically or mentally, you can be replaced. It's perceived as more cost effective to find a new person to plug into your system, rather than coach and support someone who may be suffering from burnout. The problem is this transactional approach systematically erodes trust and vulnerability within team cultures over the long term.

That's why I love the NBA and what they did during COVID. Management convinced nearly every high-profile star and player in the league to enter a bubble in Florida, which was far away from their family and in the middle of a COVID hot spot. How? Management had spent years building trust with the players by agreeing to contracts that protected the players, even when they were hurt. The players trust management to keep them safe, and management knows there is no league without great players. It's a partnership rather than the transactional relationships that exist within sales and the NFL.

In addition to providing safer contracts, the NBA is always looking to build more trust with its players. One way they did this during the pandemic was by investing further into supporting their players with their mental health, which is something all sales teams and leaders can learn from.

JUNE, Day 104: It's Showtime!

It's *showtime*! That moment when your webcam turns on for a video call, and seconds before you were raging, crying, or could barely get out of bed to face the day. This is a very real experience many of us have faced recently. When we're working from home, it's very easy to put on a mask and make things look like we're doing fine for a 30-minute call with our team or manager. Faking our emotions and wearing a mask was way harder when we had to perform for eight hours a day at the office.

Sales leaders, be mindful of the fact that not everything may be as it appears today. If you're using the happy faces on the screen staring back at you to validate that you have a "healthy" team and no one is struggling with their mental health, I hate to break it to you, but you're probably wrong. Odds are there is at least one person who is really struggling, and you're getting fooled by a great performance and a mask.

Without the physical cues and behavior changes you would normally get at the office, it's very hard to notice symptoms of declining mental health within your team. This would be a great topic to discuss as a team today because salespeople shouldn't feel like they have to put on a strong front or wear a mask when they're actually not okay.

JUNE, Day 105: The Power of Appreciation

A great leadership story that no one is talking about anymore took place in the NBA a few years ago when Chris Paul was playing for the Oklahoma City Thunder. For non-basketball fans, Chris Paul has been an all-star his entire NBA career. Before the 2019–20 season started, he was traded from an NBA title contending team (Houston Rockets) to the Oklahoma City Thunder, a team that was in rebuild mode with average talent and a team that was deemed extremely unlikely to make the playoffs. At the start of the season, the analysts initially had it right—through the first 26 games of the season they only won 12 games, a winning percentage of 46%.

Most star players would have disengaged, given up, and waited for the team to trade them. Instead, on December 17 of that year, Chris did something special. He united his team and bought each teammate a custom-tailored suit they could wear to the game, a small gesture as a leader to show his teammates he appreciated them and prove to them he had not given up. He showed he cared and invested in the people around him. The results were an 81% winning percentage over the next 11 games and their "average" team beating the top teams in the league. They went on to finish fifth in the season and one spot behind the heavily favored Houston Rockets.

As an aging veteran in the league today, he is now replicating this success with another young team in the Phoenix Suns, who finished in first place during the regular season and at the top of the Western conference in 2022.

The power of strong leadership is critical to peak performance. As a leader, keeping perspective, showing you care, and investing in the team when they least expect it is sometimes all you need to bounce back. If you're a sales leader with a struggling team, spend some time brainstorming what you can do to show genuine appreciation for the people you work with today.

JUNE, Day 106: Grab an Umbrella

When it's raining, you grab an umbrella so you don't get wet. When it's snowing, you grab a coat so you don't get cold. When you're playing football, you grab a helmet so you don't get hurt. Every single day we make choices that help protect our physical health from various environmental stressors that we expect to face in the near future. These choices help us feel comfortable, calm, safe, and ready to perform our best. So why don't we make these same choices to protect our mental health in sales?

Sales is filled with hundreds of environmental stressors that occur regularly including missing targets, dealing with angry customers, facing rejection, restarting back at zero, and buyers ghosting salespeople on important meetings. But every day, millions of salespeople wait until they're "wet," "cold," and "hurt" before they start making choices to improve their mental health. As a result, they feel anxious, stressed, overwhelmed, and more likely to underperform.

Why do you think that is? Why do most salespeople and sales leaders wait to protect their mental health? Brainstorm your reason for not prioritizing mental health and think about how you can make it easier for yourself to grab that "umbrella," "coat," or "helmet" you need to protect your mind.

JUNE, Day 107: Corporate Greed

Corporate greed and the "profits over people" mentality that exists within sales organizations need to stop. Data continues to pile up and proves things are getting worse, while companies stand idly by watching employees burn out. We all need to do our part to break this wheel of corporate greed and end the madness.

Data point #1: According to a Verizon Media white paper, "93% of managers are finding the mental health of their employees is having a negative effect on their bottom line." The bigger problem in the report is less than one third of global managers felt equipped to address the mental health needs of their teams.[1]

Data point #2: A year-long Australian population study found that full-time workers employed by organizations that fail to prioritize their employees' mental health increase their risk of being diagnosed with depression by 300%! The study explains that the root cause of this is primarily due to toxic environments and poor management.[2] Lack of recognition, unreasonable demands, providing no autonomy, bullying, and lack of support are all mentioned as management behavior that erodes the mental health and well-being of their team.

I know many of you reading this are probably not surprised by this new data, but my challenge to you is to start advocating for better mental health support at your company. Start by asking yourself the tough questions so you can become a better leader and colleague:

- Are you doing a good job supporting your own mental health?
- Do you actually know how to support your team's mental health?
- Can you recognize signs of declining mental health in others?
- Do you feel comfortable having vulnerable conversations?
- How can you use neuroscience and physiology to manage stress?
- What is stress, and how do you use it to your advantage?
- How do you effectively rest and recharge midday and mid quarter?
- Outside of this book, when did you last read, listen to a podcast, or take a course about mental health?

As a leader and compassionate teammate, we have to take responsibility for our own mental health. We have to start equipping ourselves with this knowledge if we don't already have it. We can't keep waiting for our companies to change, because even when they're losing money they're still hesitant to take initiative.

JUNE, Day 108: Learning a New Skill

I recently taught myself how to juggle. Whether it's learning to sell or any other difficult skill such as juggling, I have three best practices I use consistently to do it in a mentally healthy way:

1. **Embrace Failure**

   When learning to juggle I probably dropped the balls over 200 times. Far too often we fear failure, avoid it, and let failure take over our lives. Failure is the best teacher in the world. Embrace your teacher, and you'll surely learn from it. Learning a new skill is hard, so be compassionate to yourself. It's okay to struggle and not be perfect because everyone learns at different speeds.

2. **Intrinsic Motivation Trumps Extrinsic Motivation**

   If I was focused on an extrinsic reward such as earning money while learning to juggle, I surely would have given up. Extrinsic motivators such as money rarely get you through the tough parts of learning because when the going gets tough, it's easy for your brain to convince you to give up and find easier ways to achieve said outcomes. Intrinsic motivation is different. By believing that juggling would lead to personal growth in other areas of my life through improved hand-eye coordination, it was easy to stay motivated and connect to why it was important to keep trying to get better.

3. **The Biggest Improvement Comes after Recovery**

   When you give yourself regular breaks and time to recover, it gives your unconscious mind the time it needs to process and save everything you've learned. Every time I took a short break from juggling, I came back more capable and felt my skill level advance. This further fueled my motivation to keep learning. It's within these recovery periods where you'll experience the biggest gains in progress.

If you're in the midst of trying to learn a new sales pitch or trying to work on your copywriting for emails, try applying these best practices and see how much quicker you master the skill.

JUNE, Day 109: Be Like Mike

As I watched Michael Jordan's *The Last Dance* on Netflix, one observation continues to remain clear. The greats, whether it be in sports or business, have rewired their brains so their desire to win far outweighs their fear of losing. For most of us, normal folk, the opposite is true and our fear of losing is greater than our desire to win. Evolution has wired us to fear losing more than we enjoy gains because if we lose too much, it leads to death. Gains on the other hand feel really good when they happen but have diminishing returns.

This phenomenon was proven by Daniel Kahneman, who studied the bias humans have toward loss aversion.[3] If you think about this situation rationally, winning $100 should be as equally pleasurable as losing $100 is painful. Kahneman proved this not to be true, and what he uncovered through his experiments was losing $100 bothers us *a lot* more than winning $100 makes us feel good. Our bias to prioritize loss aversion over gains is likely affecting many areas of our lives in a negative way. For example, this bias can motivate us to stay with people and companies that make us unhappy or avoid difficult tasks outside our comfort zone simply because it means we won't lose—even if there is a great opportunity to win by taking on some risk to land our dream job.

The greats have learned to rewire this bias and change their perspective so their desire to win is much greater than their fear of loss. This also helps them use losing as a positive motivator to learn and grow, which helps them come back better and win the next time. That's how they became great and is a helpful road map for all of us to follow in the face of adversity.

JUNE, Day 110: What Are You Feeling?

When we feel ourselves getting upset or see others who are anxious or stressed, we need to stop asking, "What's wrong?" Instead, we should be asking, "What are you feeling?"

Our society conditions us to ask others, "What's wrong?" because it is the quickest way to identify a problem so we can provide a solution: "Do X, and you'll feel better," or "Take Y, and you'll feel better." Problem solved. Easy.

Mental health doesn't work in this way, and often when we're feeling anxious or depressed, nothing is actually wrong. We usually use words such as "I'm anxious" or "I'm depressed" as catch-all phrases when we're having a difficult time identifying and processing the vulnerable emotions we're feeling. Society doesn't teach us how to properly label emotions such as fear, guilt, grief, anger, embarrassment, shame, and countless other difficult emotions that come up regularly when working in sales. We're conditioned to think that having these emotions is wrong or weak, which means before we can learn what they actually feel like, we're already burying them deep inside ourselves.

But having these emotions is *normal*, and they make us human. Next time someone on your team is struggling, avoid asking what's wrong. Get curious and ask them about what they're feeling because usually the only thing that's "wrong" is they're having trouble making sense of the emotions swirling around inside.

JUNE Endnotes

1. Brodey, D. "93% of Managers Watch as Mental Health Negatively Impacts Bottom Line." *Forbes.* June 21, 2021. https://www.forbes.com/sites/denisebrodey/2021/06/21/93-of-managers-watch-as-mental-health-negatively-impacts-bottom-line/?sh=302851931bf9.
2. University of South Australia. "Toxic workplaces increase risk of depression by 300%." EurekAlert. June 23, 2021. https://www.eurekalert.org/news-releases/708076.
3. Grant, H. "The Hidden Danger of Being Risk-Averse." *Harvard Business Review.* July 2, 2013. https://hbr.org/2013/07/hidden-danger-of-being-risk-averse.

JULY

JULY, Day 111: Back from Vacation

The first day back from vacation can be filled with overwhelming feelings of fear, anxiety, and self-doubt. Here are four tips to help you get started on the right foot and protect your mental health upon returning.

1. Pick Three

You likely have too many items on your to-do list. If you could only accomplish three tasks today, which three tasks would make you feel the most accomplished at the end of the day? Block your calendar and do those three things.

2. Shutdown Time

Before you start working today, decide what time you're going to switch off. No matter what happens today and how much work is left unfinished, stick to that shutdown time. Start fresh after vacation by building stronger boundaries with work.

3. "I Get To"

You're probably saying to yourself, "I *have* to do X, Y, and Z today." Instead, change your mindset to "I *get* to do X, Y, and Z today." Thousands of job seekers are fighting to have the opportunity to do X, Y, and Z. Be grateful that you *get* the opportunity to do them.

4. Eat Right

We all overindulge while on vacation, which means part of the reason why we're experiencing brain fog and moving slowly is all the extra fat, sugar, and alcohol we put into our bodies. Get back to healthy eating habits, and make sure you're fueling your body with nutrient-rich food to get your mind and body running smoothly again.

If you have a vacation planned in the near future, make sure you set a reminder to revisit this page on the day you get back.

JULY, Day 112: Your Signature Move

Do you have a "signature move" in sales? All the great athletes have a signature move, and so should you. Michael Jordan had a fade-away. Kareem Abdul-Jabbar had a skyhook. Tim Duncan had a bank shot. Ronda Rousey had an armbar. Muhammed Ali had his "shuffle." Serena Williams has her serve.

These signature moves became iconic, because even though the opponents knew what to expect, there was nothing they could do to stop them. This meant if the athletes above were ever feeling flustered or overwhelmed by a high-pressure moment or setback, they had a signature move they could depend on. They could use one of their unique strengths or skills to help them rebuild their confidence and shift momentum in their direction.

Working in sales is no different, and salespeople are corporate athletes who face pressures and setbacks every single day. That's why each salesperson needs to have a signature move, something that is unstoppable (can be used at any time) and uses individual strengths to build confidence and repair self-esteem when facing adversity. First step to creating a signature move is to identify your unique strengths and skills, so here are some questions to help you get started:

1. What do other people tell you you're good at?
2. What types of activities or hobbies bring you joy?
3. When have you spent hours working on something without feeling tired?
4. What work tasks do you enjoy in sales that don't often feel like work?
5. Last time something went wrong, what skills did you use to resolve it?

Journaling about these five questions should help you identify a solid list of activities, strengths, and skills that give you energy. You then want to brainstorm how you can complete more of these tasks and use these strengths more frequently on a daily basis. More importantly, you want to think about building a signature move and create a tool you can use to help protect your mental health and motivation after encountering a nasty stressor such as losing a deal.

Remember a signature move has two components: (1) It can be used at any time (not really dependent on others), and (2) it requires the use of your strengths or unique skills. For example, let's say you've identified that you're good at making people laugh, creative, and love making GIFs on Instagram. Well, next time you're feeling unmotivated after receiving a slew of "Not interested" email responses from prospects, spend 15 minutes creating a new GIF about the challenges your prospects face, something that will make them laugh and can be included in future cold emails (signature move). Alternatively, maybe you've identified that you really like reading books, experimenting with new ideas, and building processes. Well, next time you're feeling sluggish and bored with the repetition of calling leads, pause and read 10 pages of a new sales book. Then apply something you learned such as a new question you can ask on your next call (signature move).

Remember your signature move is a quick action you can take to shift momentum toward a more positive mood. They're designed to help you build confidence and repair your self-esteem when you're feeling defeated, not procrastinate for hours on something that will put you further behind.

JULY, Day 113: Empowering Sales Teams

A question I often get asked by sales leaders is, "How do you empower your sales team without micromanaging them?" My suggestion is to always focus on filling these four buckets consistently that Scott Barry Kaufman highlights in his book *Transcend*[1]:

Bucket 1: Safety

Managing through fear does *not* work—period. Retention will always be an issue, and managing through fear keeps reps anxious. Without job security, reps will never be able to learn, experiment, and grow.

Bucket 2: Self-Esteem

Salespeople consistently encounter experiences that challenge their self-esteem. It's easy to start thinking, "I'm a failure" in sales. When these experiences occur, leaders must remind their reps of the learning, growth, and progress within adversity.

Bucket 3: Connection

Fostering connection between team members helps create a strong sense of belonging. Creating a safe space for vulnerable discussions around mental health can help build strong bonds of trust and supportive relationships between colleagues.

Bucket 4: Meaning

Everyone wants to be part of something bigger than themselves. When reps lose perspective and metrics become meaningless, leaders need to remind them of the greater purpose behind their work. Remind them how achieving metrics is tied to helping the customers they serve and the personal goals they're working toward.

JULY, Day 114: Top-Down, Bottom-Up

There are a lot of mindset sales coaches putting out some amazing content right now, but improving your mindset is just one part of bettering your overall sales performance and mental health.

Mindset is defined as a collection of beliefs, attitudes, and opinions *toward* yourself and the world around you. These beliefs, attitudes, and opinions will direct where you focus your attention and your thoughts. Simple example, you've just lost a deal. If you believe losing a deal is dangerous and will lead to you getting fired, then you're more likely to focus on the negative and threatening aspects of losing a deal. If you believe losing a deal is a setback that you can learn from, then you're more likely to focus on the learning and growth opportunities that losing a deal provides.

The best part is we can change our mindset by injecting new beliefs, attitudes, and opinions into our thought pattern that will help us become resilient to stressors by perceiving them in a more positive light. Often these new beliefs, attitudes, and opinions will be classified into buckets such as growth mindset, abundance mindset, curiosity mindset, or solutions-oriented mindset. Mindset coaches will teach you how to use these strategies effectively and interrupt negative thinking patterns.

The shortcomings of these mindset strategies is they're a *top-down* approach to controlling stress and our emotions. This means using these new mindsets to reframe and reshape how we're perceiving our environment requires the use of our prefrontal cortex. This is the part of our brain that is responsible for logic, creativity, rational thinking, and implementing our mindset strategies. The problem is using this part of our brain requires *a lot* of energy. That's why it's easy to tell yourself, "It's going to be an *amazing* day" and feel optimistic in the morning but then feel defeated, unmotivated, and negative by the end of the day when we're tired. The prefrontal cortex is out of energy and powering down, which is making it hard to lead with the right mindset.

Yes mindset strategies will keep this prefrontal cortex online longer, but if we're working in a toxic environment, suffering from trauma, experiencing burnout, having trouble sleeping, or not using our energy efficiently throughout the day, then our mindset will erode, become less resilient, and break down.

Top-down mindset strategies are extremely important, but learning *bottom-up* strategies that show us how to use our physiology to help us shutdown our stress response is equally as important to feeling and performing our best each day. They also help protect our mindset.

 Resilience requires having both top-down and bottom-up strategies in your toolkit, which I teach virtually to sales teams. Scan here to see the list of programs I offer to companies.

JULY, Day 115: Eustress vs Distress

Understanding how stress works is a critical component of building resilience and performing at a high level in sales. What most people don't understand about stress is it operates on a spectrum. "Eustress" is defined as positive stress, which helps us feel challenged, focused, and energized, whereas negative stress is called "distress" and happens when stress levels get too high and push us toward fatigue, exhaustion, and burnout.

When you work out at the gym and you feel sore the next day, that's eustress. Your muscles have been pushed outside their comfort zone to grow, and you're taking the necessary time to allow them to recover. In this scenario, distress occurs when muscles are not given appropriate time to recover. They get pushed too hard to grow too quickly, leading to injury.

Same rules apply to your mental health and sales. An achievable but challenging sales target that pushes you outside your comfort zone is a good thing. Eustress pushes you to grow and stay motivated. Poorly set targets or encountering some negative experiences such as a few deals falling through can often leave you behind and grinding to the finish line. This is distress, and you need to be mindful of when this happens and when stress becomes negative. In situations when you're operating in distress, take the steps you need to recover before your next target.

Managers and organizations need to be mindful of the sales reps who are operating in distress for long periods of time because mental health and performance are being affected. Look for ways to give them quota relief or an extra self-care day so they can recover and come back stronger.

Today try scheduling two additional 15-minute breaks into your day, where you totally disconnect from work and social media by going outside. Put them on your calendar so you don't miss them, and see how you feel at the end of the day. My guess is this small change will help you feel more challenged, energized, and productive.

JULY, Day 116: Benefits of Meditation

Are you curious about meditation? Maybe you have tried meditating but couldn't stick with it? Or maybe this is a skill you practice regularly? Meditation has been a foundational piece of caring for my mental health and self-care on a daily basis.

A study from 2012 showed that after only eight weeks of mindfulness meditation, participants showed reduced activity in part of the brain called the amygdala.[2] This is part of our emotional brain that is responsible for detecting threats and helps manage our emotional response to danger. What this means is meditation can help us be less emotionally reactive to stressors we face within sales. It can also limit how much time our mind spends glued to any negative thoughts they elicit. Several other studies have shown that meditation enlarges and strengthens various other areas of our brain such as the prefrontal cortex. Strengthening this part of our brain improves our:

- Emotional self-awareness;
- Self-regulation, or impulse control;
- Ability to focus our attention;
- Compassion toward others.

Much like an athlete who works out to strengthen their muscles to prevent injury and perform well during a physical sport, meditating is literally a workout for our brain, which allows us to strengthen the areas of our mind that we need to:

- Sell effectively;
- Build mental resilience to stressors that affect mental health;
- Feel in control of our emotions while under stress.

The problem is meditation can be extremely tough to get into, and most platforms only offer a seven-day trial, which is not nearly enough to build a new habit. We need support, flexibility, and compassion getting to at least that eight-week mark where the research says we'll start experiencing real benefits. That's why my favorite meditation tool is the Balance app because they tailor their meditations to your experience level, and last time I checked, they provide a one-year free trial to give you adequate time to build a good meditation habit before paying. Check them out!

JULY, Day 117: Emotional Literacy

Sales can feel like an emotional roller coaster, but it feels this way because most salespeople are "emotionally illiterate." This means we have a really tough time labeling how we're feeling and putting our emotions into words that describe them.

When we are unable to label and describe what we're feeling internally, it scares us and can make our emotions feel overwhelming. It can also put us in a situation where we're only able to describe ("only literate in") really powerful emotions such as anger, joy, sadness, and anxiety. If we're only able to label the more powerful emotions, it can leave us ping ponging between really *high* highs and really *low* lows. This is why a lot of salespeople describe working within sales as an "emotional roller coaster," where our emotions go up and down very quickly.

When we can't identify and communicate our emotions to others, they tend to get bundled up and trapped inside us. Over time this will start to affect our mental health, relationships, and sales performance because internal emotional turmoil is extremely uncomfortable. The article below should help you improve your emotional literacy and help you identify what emotions you're feeling throughout the day so you can release them more consistently and mitigate the peaks and valleys of the emotional roller coaster.

Scan here to give it a read: "The Emotional Roller Coaster in Sales."

JULY, Day 118: Compound Resilience

Mental resilience is quickly becoming a popular topic within sales teams, but most sales reps and leaders are taking the wrong approach. This becomes clear when we look at how the average salesperson is using recovery periods to manage stress within their role. We can see the pitfall in their approach when we understand the interdependence between stress, resilience, and recovery. To do this, we can ask ourselves a simple question: Would you rather have $1 today that doubles each day for a month or $1 million one time?

Many of you were probably asked this question in grade seven or eight when your math teacher told you "The Grain of Rice" fable to teach you about the value of compound interest. If you haven't heard this fable before, the math behind taking $1 a day that doubles works out like this:

Day 1 – $1

Day 2 – $2

Day 7 – $64

Day 15 – $16,384

Day 21 – $1,048,576

Day 30 – $536,870,912

Over the 30-day period you will have made almost $1 billion. This exercise will likely get any elementary school student excited to start saving and investing their money, but the same compounding effect should get any adult or company excited about something called:

Compound mental resilience. This is the benefit in performance and overall well-being that is created by investing time into restoring and protecting your mental health daily, rather than occasionally throughout the year.

When a salesperson relies too heavily on taking vacations to manage their stress levels, or companies lean on wellness days, this is similar to taking the $1 million up front. They provide a ton of value and offload stress across the entire organization, but they require more vacations and wellness days (more time) in the future when the "$1 million" runs out, aka when stress levels become unmanageable again. Between vacations and wellness days, sales performance is also steadily declining as elevated stress levels chip away at mental health.

Instead, when organizations and individuals invest "$1 of time" into supporting their mental health on a daily basis, their mental resilience to stress compounds over time to raise baseline well-being and performance levels. This is what any good resilience and mental health training program should help you do: teach you how to invest and maximize that "$1 of time" each day by showing you how to self-regulate your stress levels and become more resilient to the unique stressors you face *every* day. With a proper toolkit you can create a happier, healthier, and more productive version of yourself that exponentially improves over time.

JULY, Day 119: Block the Sales Dashboard

Are you up for this challenge? Try blocking your sales dashboard for the entire day. Sales teams are obsessed with achieving outcomes, which leads us to asking the wrong question over and over again: How are we doing? How are we doing *compared* to previous days? How are we doing *compared* to future sales targets? How are we doing *compared* to our teammates? As a result, we become too focused on the *past*, the *future*, and on *other* people. This makes it nearly impossible to focus on solving current challenges and executing on the *present* task (call, email, etc.) to the best of our ability.

Stop comparing, and instead start asking: "*What* are we doing right now?" Research shows when we're less distracted by rewards and punishments that are tied to outcomes (i.e. sales metrics), we experience boosts in performance, learning, memory, creativity, problem solving, resilience, and mental health and make less mistakes in the present moment. Sales targets and metrics are important, but looking at them 20 times or more a day will have detrimental effects. If you want to take a break from your sales dashboard, here is how you can temporarily block it:

Step 1: Add the Chrome extension BlockSite.

Step 2: Take your unique Sales Dashboard URL from Salesforce or Hubspot and add it to the blocked sites list.

You'll still be able to use your CRM but won't be able to check the dashboard until you no longer have it as a blocked site.

JULY, Day 120: Upper Limit Happiness

You've just closed a massive deal, and you feel invincible, but then all of a sudden you're hit with a wave of self-doubt and negative self-talk. In her book *The Wisdom of Anxiety*, Sheryl Paul describes this as "upper limit happiness," which is anxiety that prevents us from enjoying positive emotions during happy moments in our lives.[3]

We often connect anxiety to situations, emotions, or events that are perceived as negative or make us uncomfortable. When we encounter these threatening situations, we start to feel anxious because our ego is trying to protect us and avoid something it perceives as dangerous. But the same process can happen during moments of peak happiness as well, when we close a big deal, fall in love, or we land our dream job. These are extremely vulnerable moments your ego can also perceive as dangerous because all of a sudden you now have something to *lose*. Your internal dialogue may switch to, "You just got lucky," "You don't deserve to be with them," or "You can't actually do that job."

When this switch happens and negative internal chatter takes over, acknowledge that it is just anxiety. You did in fact just do something so incredibly awesome that you scared the sh*t out of that voice inside your head. Thank your little guardian ego, and journal about why you're scared. Also write down three things you're grateful for in what you just accomplished. This will keep the good vibes flowing and help you get back to the present so you can enjoy the moment.

JULY, Day 121: The Right Action

"Actions change first . . . then thoughts . . . then feelings . . . and in that order. We can't force our feelings to change. They follow our thoughts, which follow our actions." This was a powerful rule shared by Olympian Alexi Pappas on an episode of the *Rich Roll* podcast talking about mental health.[4]

On paper this seems simple enough to follow, but in reality it's far more difficult to execute consistently for three primary reasons:

1. **We have trouble *labeling* our feelings:**
   Do you know how your own mind and body expresses feeling stressed, anxious, overwhelmed, depressed, lonely, bored, frustrated, scared, or any of the other emotions we can face on a daily basis in sales? Especially after experiencing a stressor, such as missing our sales target or losing our job, we can be faced with several intense and unfamiliar emotions simultaneously. When we can't label these emotions, our *feelings* get heavier, our brain gets stuck *thinking* and over-analyzing, while our *actions* get paralyzed. If we can't label what we're feeling internally, then we likely won't know what action to take to feel better.

2. **We *neglect* our thoughts and feelings:**
   Maybe we think exploring our emotions shows weakness? Maybe we don't think mental health is important? Maybe our thoughts and feelings scare us so we avoid them? Or maybe we're so distracted and/or addicted to other areas of our life (social media, work, drugs, sex, fame, etc.) that we never spend time exploring our inner world? Whatever the reason, neglecting the hidden messages and needs of our inner world will always affect the actions we take in the external world.

3. **We take the *wrong* actions too often:**
   We overwork, stay up too late, have too much to drink, wake up too early, or we play too much. It's normal to get caught up in the moment and overdo it from time to time. That's called being human. But if we consistently take the wrong actions too often (aka bad habits), then they'll start to change our thoughts and then our feelings—for the worse.

As you go about your day, which of the three reasons above are holding you back from taking the *right action* you need to start *thinking* and *feeling* better today?

JULY, Day 122: Hearing vs Listening

Do you know the difference between hearing and listening? On a hot summer day in 2020, I was reminded of how easy it is to become grounded in the moment when you simply *listen* to sounds in your environment. I was sitting on my bike waiting for the light to change at an intersection I've stopped at hundreds of times before. Then all of a sudden the bells of the church next to me started to ring as the clock struck noon. I'd *heard* these bells many times before, but this time I *listened*.

As I listened to their simple melody, I found myself in awe. I was in awe by the fact that these bells have been ringing every single day for way longer than I had been alive. I was in awe thinking of these massive bells being hoisted up to the top of the church with limited technology. I was in awe now knowing that their sound and beauty is hidden behind the hum of traffic and that few stop to listen. More importantly as I listened to the bells ring, I realized I was totally present. I wasn't worried about starting my work week or what I had to do next. I was consumed by the moment and any anxious thoughts were gone.

This experience was a simple reminder that beauty can be found anywhere, even at a red light in the middle of traffic in busy downtown Toronto. All it takes is a little effort to stop, look, and truly listen to your environment—a perfect cure for anxiety.

JULY, Day 123: Distanced from Work

One burnout symptom that usually gets misperceived in sales is feeling increased mental distance from one's job or feeling negative toward one's career. This symptom will have a direct impact on motivation and sales performance.

When sales reps start feeling this way, it can be easy for them to start thinking they're in the wrong company, career, or role. If they get left thinking this way for too long, it can start to feel like they're trapped or being suffocated, which fuels more anxiety that they need to change something immediately to find relief. That's why a sales rep working in a great environment but struggling with burnout might unexpectedly quit for no apparent reason.

Sales leaders, recognize this is likely happening to people on your team. If someone is disengaged, don't assume they are lazy, checked out, or bad at sales. They likely just need your help creating a safe space to openly talk about how they're feeling. Then you can help them reconnect with their goals, purpose, and values in the work they are doing. Start by bringing attention to this burnout symptom today so you can find out who needs some additional support.

JULY, Day 124: Competing Perspectives in Sales

It's important to acknowledge that most CROs and VPs of sales are too far removed from the front lines to be able to set sales targets effectively on their own. They have all of the control but often lack direct feedback on how customers and salespeople are doing overall. Salespeople, on the other hand, have all of the customer and peer feedback but none of the control.

In his book *Leaders Eat Last*, Simon Sinek explains that this difference in perspective and control can lead to something called destructive abundance.[5] This is when leaders become selfish and start to put their individual goals (individual bonuses) ahead of more selfless goals that benefit salespeople several corporate rungs below them but not the leader directly. The further removed leaders are from the front lines, the more isolated their perspective becomes. Salespeople become numbers and statistics on a spreadsheet as the connection and empathy toward individual employees is lost through multiple layers of corporate structure.

This causes people at the top to prioritize results *over* the people generating those results. It leads to creating dopamine-centric incentives and bonus structures as the backbone of motivation, rather than instilling true connection with the purpose of the work. With too much dopamine flowing through an organization, individuals and leaders become selfish as a "me first" culture is created. This is the type of culture that is very fragile to change (COVID, recessions, etc.) because periods of great change require individuals from top to bottom to work together.

One way to resolve destructive abundance within sales is to inject more collaboration into the sales target setting process, by giving salespeople more input. I explore how smaller sales teams can do this, so scan the QR code to give the article a read.

JULY, Day 125: Top Performers

The similarities between a high-performing athlete in sports and the best salespeople in an organization is astounding. They both require an individual to consistently perform their craft to near perfection, while under high pressure and facing adversity.

One of the major differences between the two, however, is how they approach the mental game. Whether it's basketball, golf, or any other sport, performance experts, coaches, and athletes all know that they will be unable to perform their craft at a high level if their mental health suffers. When they're anxious, experiencing self-doubt, or overwhelmed by the moment, they become unfocused, make mistakes, and lose their edge. Even the most physically gifted athletes will suffer if they lack the mental resilience to keep their mind sharp under stress. That's why the best athletes know that the key to having a long career revolves around protecting both their mind and body.

Now some of the best athletes, more than ever, are starting to speak more openly about mental health. Naomi Osaka, Simone Biles, Demar DeRozan, and Paul George are just a few that are paving the way for others. There are many lessons the sales industry can learn from these athletes with the main one being even the best salespeople need mental health support. Today, check in on those on your team who are performing well to make sure they're okay mentally.

JULY, Day 126: The Bus Stop

One of the most memorable things a sales leader said to me as a rep was, "This role and company might just be a bus stop—and that's okay."

I heard this sage advice when I was 1½ years into an account executive role at a great company and making good money. But it just didn't feel right. The sizzle of working at a "cool start-up" had worn off, and I knew I was missing something. I realized I hadn't learned anything in six months, and it felt like I was just going through the motions of everyday life. I felt like if I wasn't careful, I'd wake up five years from where I was and still be the same person, someone who hadn't grown personally or professionally but with a little extra cash in their pocket and some material possessions.

In response to the discomfort and anxiety I was feeling about the lack of growth, there was tension with my new manager. I was asking her for unrealistic demands such as a better career path, more leadership opportunities, and new ways to grow in a short period of time. To be honest, I was being a total ass to someone who had just started herself. I was unwilling to accept that large companies are process driven, move slowly, and oftentimes, company politics plays a huge part in who gets ahead, a frustrating game I thought I could change.

Then one day, in a tense meeting with my new manager, Madalina, she dropped her wisdom: "This role and company might just be a bus stop—and that's okay." Immediately everything became clear. I realized that this *is* a bus stop, and it's time to move on. I had outgrown my company, and I was scared to give up the safety and comfort of a good job. More importantly, it allowed my manager and I to have a better understanding of each other's needs, which eased our tension. I had more clarity and could feel comfortable exploring new companies, while she could start looking for a new salesperson to replace me without being blindsided.

Lesson of the story: You may not be in your dream job or dream company, but that's okay. Bus stops are an important part of getting you to where you need to go. Just make sure you enjoy them, work hard, be kind to others, learn what you can, and don't stay too long. Personal growth and fulfillment is waiting for you at your next destination.

JULY, Day 127: Overtraining

Sales enablement folks, are you getting frustrated because your training, coaching, and resources that you spend hours developing are not sticking? If learning retention is a problem with your sales teams, then you're most likely *overtraining* them, and burnout is causing them to plateau.

Sales enablement invests 100% of their time and effort primarily into improving areas in sales such as higher volume metrics, conversion metrics, output metrics (deal size, sales velocity, etc.), and developing sales rep skills (negotiation, objection handling, etc.). These areas make up your sales enablement "cart" of processes, tools, and strategies. What most enablers fail to realize is that the horse—aka the salesperson—comes *before* the cart. If the horse (salesperson) is unwell, then the cart will never move optimally. Overtraining leads to burnout, which makes them unwell.

If you're working in sales enablement, it's absolutely critical you start investing an *equal* amount of time training your sales team in areas such as mental health, resilience, stress-management, physical health, and sleep. Many HR folks are trying to tackle these areas but have no idea what it's like to work in sales. It's on you in sales enablement to act as the bridge between HR and sales. This is your training insurance policy and how you actually *enable sellers* to reach peak performance.

JULY, Day 128: Afternoon Coffee

How good does an afternoon coffee feel on days when we're tired? Pretty amazing right? Unfortunately, it might be time to rethink this decision because the afternoon coffee may actually be making your mental health worse and less resilient to stress in sales. It does this by masking our sleep deprivation with caffeine.

In his book *Why We Sleep*, Matthew Walker explains how when we are sleep deprived, the emotional part of our brain (amygdala) becomes extremely difficult to control and takes over our thinking.[6] In fact, studies show there is well over a 60% amplification in emotional reactivity in participants who are sleep deprived.[7] When the amygdala is hyperactive, it becomes easy for us to react irrationally and get irritated by small events that happen in our environment. Not only are we hypersensitive to events in our environment when we're sleep deprived, we also have a tough time controlling our desires. We become more impulsive because another region of the brain that is responsible for driving our bad habits, addictions, and pleasure-seeking activities such as overeating also becomes more active.

To make matters worse, the prefrontal cortex (the logical part of the brain), which we learned about earlier, is tired. In well-rested individuals, the prefrontal cortex is responsible for controlling our emotions. After a few nights of bad sleep and our logical brain snoozing, lost deals in sales start to feel more overwhelming, rejection feels more personal, and a buyer who is unresponsive becomes the bane of our existence.

One easy way to combat this from happening is to ditch the afternoon coffee, which is silently disrupting our sleep and pushing us further toward sleep deprivation. The problem with caffeine in the afternoon is it takes a long time for your metabolism to remove it from your body. For example, if you have an afternoon coffee at 3 p.m., the average person will still have roughly 50% of the caffeine in their system by 8–10 p.m. As a result, we'll feel less pressure to go to sleep at a reasonable time, and even if we make the smart decision to go to bed, the stages of sleep (deep sleep and REM) we need to quiet our amygdala and refuel our prefrontal cortex are likely to be affected by lingering caffeine.

Today, rather than reaching for an afternoon coffee, try replacing it with a 15 minute meditation or 30 minute nap instead. Though you won't feel the immediate boost in wakefulness a coffee will provide (caffeine is a very powerful drug), these activities should provide you with enough extra energy to push through the day and set you up for a better night's rest. With a good recovery, you'll be better prepared to crush your sales tasks the next day.

JULY, Day 129: Email Apnea

Thanks to James Nestor's book *Breath*, I learned that up to 80% of us can suffer from something called "email apnea".[8] It happens when we become so distracted by an email that our breathing becomes erratic or we stop breathing altogether. Sometimes we stop breathing for 30 seconds or more, and it contributes to the same issues caused by sleep apnea. But it doesn't just apply to emails, and when salespeople are operating in a continuous state of distraction, they unconsciously stop breathing. They're so distracted as they move from LinkedIn to Slack messages and then to a last-minute client request that they simply forget to breathe.

This is what email apnea feels like when it happens: We get distracted and stop breathing → CO_2 builds up in our system → Our breathing then restarts at a faster pace taking short, quick breaths to try and remove the excess CO_2 → Then our heart rate speeds up because of the short quick inhales we just took, and all of a sudden we're feeling a sense of panic and we don't even know why. Panic that can affect our performance for the rest of the day.

Remember the process above happens unconsciously, which means it's unlikely we'll be aware of when it's happening until it's too late. Today, try scheduling a 10-minute meditation at lunch so you can reset your body and breathing in the middle of the day. One of my favorites is an *equal breathing breath practice* that involves simply inhaling for five seconds and then exhaling for five seconds throughout the entire duration of your meditation. This will help you consciously reconnect with your breath and stabilize your breathing pattern.

JULY, Day 130: Theory X or Theory Y

Do you subscribe to Theory X or Theory Y as a sales leader? This was a theory created by MIT professor Douglas McGregor during the 1960s to explain two management approaches in business.[9]

Theory X sales managers believe that salespeople primarily work because you pay them and provide a good commission structure. As a result, when salespeople fall behind pace and higher commissions become less attainable, you have to keep watching them or they stop working. Theory Y sales managers, on the other hand, believe salespeople are intrinsically motivated by the satisfaction they get in helping their clients improve through the products and services they sell. As a result, they work more effectively with the freedom to creatively problem-solve during tough months and require less daily supervision.

The reason this theory is important is because a leader's mindset (X or Y) toward their team matters. Studies have shown that managers who believe Theory X usually have employees that need constant supervision, while managers who believe Theory Y usually have employees who love the work they do. Though lucrative commission checks can be motivating, Theory X runs the risk of placing too much focus on outcomes, which can often be uncontrollable in sales. As a leader, by shifting your focus to Theory Y, you foster greater resilience and better mental health in your team by making work more meaningful. Sellers then have a better opportunity to fall in love with the process of selling and helping others.

JULY Endnotes

1. Kaufman, S. B. (2021). *Transcend: The new science of self-actualization.* J.P. Tarcher, U.S./Perigee Bks.
2. Powell, A. "When Science Meets Mindfulness." *The Harvard Gazette.* April 9, 2018. https://news.harvard.edu/gazette/story/2018/04/harvard-researchers-study-how-mindfulness-may-change-the-brain-in-depressed-patients/.
3. Paul, S. (2019). *The Wisdom of Anxiety: How Worry and Intrusive Thoughts Are Gifts to Help You Heal.* Sounds True.
4. Roll, R. "Mastering the Mind: A Mental Health Deep Dive." *Rich Roll* podcast. July 8, 2021. https://youtu.be/mnH_Y5bxbPY.
5. Sinek, S. (2017). *Leaders Eat Last: Why some teams pull together and others don't.* Portfolio Penguin.
6. Walker, M. (2018). *Why We Sleep.* Penguin Books.
7. Yoo, S.S., Gujar, N., Hu, P., Jolesz, F.A., and Walker, M.P. "The human emotional brain without sleep—a prefrontal amygdala disconnect." *Current Biology.* 2007;17:R877–8.
8. Nestor, J. (2021). *Breath: The new science of a lost art.* Da Kuai Wen Hua.
9. McGregor, D. "The human side of enterprise." *Classics of Organization Theory,* 1966.

AUGUST

AUGUST, Day 131: Uncoupling from Fear

Failure in sales can strike *fear* into salespeople; however, leaders can play an important role in helping reps uncouple fear from failure.

One way you can achieve this as a leader is each month start by selecting one or two members on your sales team to throw the sales playbook out and run an experiment. Tell them to get creative and to try something totally different from the current sales process they are executing on. This can be writing a new script or email sequence, prospecting a different vertical, running a different demo, or trying something old-school such as direct-mailing gifts to prospects. The more creative, the better. Then, have them present the key learning and results of the experiment to the team at the end of the month.

But there is an important key to making this work: pay the salespeople their *full* base salary and commission, regardless of whether or not the experiment is successful. The point of the experiment is *not* to hit target. The point is to *learn* through failure. To innovate, move the entire team forward and create an environment where failure is embraced, provided something is learned from it. As a leader, when you reward intelligent failures consistently, you create a supportive environment with more autonomy and trust, which leads to better mental health.

AUGUST, Day 132: Courageous Vulnerability

To the hardened salesperson and sales leader who believes sales is no place for vulnerability and mental health, I'm going to change your mind with one question I learned from Brené Brown in her book *Dare to Lead.*[1] To preface this question, think about the most courageous moments in your life like when:

> You made that big presentation;
>
> You took that shot with the game on the line;
>
> You called that decision maker six pay grades higher than you;
>
> You finally asked your crush out;
>
> You went in for that surgery;
>
> You quit and left that toxic environment;
>
> You took that job you were underqualified for;
>
> You stood up to that bully.

During all of these courageous moments in your life, were you being vulnerable and putting yourself in a situation where you might be emotionally hurt, judged, shamed, or physically harmed?

The answer is undeniably yes.

The greatest moments of strength and courage come from the greatest moments of vulnerability. Next time you think emotions and vulnerability are a sign of weakness in sales, remember to come back to this page. Recognize the strength and courage in those salespeople on your team who are being vulnerable.

AUGUST, Day 133: Mindset Matters

If you go looking for reasons to believe you are a failure in sales, you will find them. Just like if you go looking for reasons to believe you are growing in sales, you will also find them.

This is because our mindset is a collection of beliefs, attitudes, and opinions *toward* ourselves and our environment. It shapes and influences our perception, which is a collection of beliefs, attitudes, and opinions *about* ourselves and our environment. Our mindset is directing our senses (sight, hearing, touch, smell, and taste) and telling them what to put more attention on in our environment. Here's an example of our mindset in action:

Mindset 1: "I love dogs." It becomes easy to pick out and perceive a dog on a busy street because it is an enjoyable experience for us.

Mindset 2: "I think dogs are dangerous." It becomes easy to pick out and perceive a dog on a busy street because it is a threat to you and an experience you want to avoid.

Mindset 3: "I don't care about dogs—I like birds." You probably won't even perceive the dog but notice the bird flying through the air.

Three different mindsets, driving three different perspectives, in exactly the same moment of time. This is why adopting a gratitude practice can help change our perception from "this was a bad day" to "this was a good day" because it makes it easier to perceive all the positive experiences happening around us every single day.

AUGUST, Day 134: Praising Effort and Learning

I was asked a great question by a person in my network recently: "What does a quota do to the mental health of salespeople?"

When quotas are set properly and the sales rep is supported, they provide a meaningful goal that can result in an incredibly rewarding experience, a positive mental health experience that helps build resilience through personal and professional growth. Quotas become problematic when sales teams believe they are not allowed to fail and the only outcome that is praised or rewarded is achieving quota. Sales is a journey, and equal praise needs to be given to the effort and learning that went into their work, regardless of the outcome. If the effort, learning, and growth is there, then *praise* it.

Failure is one of the best teachers, but if we fear it, we can't learn from it. It's the same as telling two basketball players they have to make 18 out of 20 free throws. One player you threaten with a punishment if they fail to sink enough free throws and then you criticize them after each basket (outcome) they miss. The other player you focus on praising their effort and learning, while providing feedback on what they can improve after every shot they miss. Both may not hit 18/20 free throws, but the second player will certainly "achieve target" quicker and more consistently than the first player over time. Today, practice *praising* yourself and colleagues for *effort* and *learning*, regardless of what the outcomes may be.

AUGUST, Day 135: Perception and Targets

When sales targets get set, there is one important question all sales leaders need to ask themselves: "How will each sales rep on my team perceive their target?"

Too often sales targets get set and sales leaders only consider whether the target is achievable from their own perspective. Then they get to work managing performance to their perspective. As a result they often miss how sales targets are being perceived by their team. This can lead to declining mental health and performance issues.

In Mihaly Csikszentmihalyi's book *Flow* he states[2]: "Enjoyment (in sales) appears at the boundary between boredom and anxiety, when the challenges of a task (sales target) are just balanced with the person's capacity and ability to act." The boundary Mihaly is talking about is usually a matter of perception.

The same task (sales target) can be seen as too easy, too challenging, or impossible by three different reps. Asking the question above forces sales leaders to consider their reps' perspective and to see the sales target from the reps' eyes. In doing so they'll be able to adjust their management style to better support those who may be overwhelmed or anxious and work with them to regain perspective, to help them enjoy their work (in sales) by seeing it as challenging but achievable.

AUGUST, Day 136: Becoming a CEO

If you're struggling with your mental health today, think about how you can become a better CEO, a better *Chief Energy Officer*.

Jan Muhlfeit shared this term in his book *The Positive Leader* and explains how managing our daily energy is critical to helping us *respond* rather than *react* to situations.[3] *Responding* to situations means we're using the logical part of our human brain (prefrontal cortex), that helps us keep perspective and achieve the best possible outcomes, interactions, and decisions within sales. When we're *reacting* to situations in sales, it means our highly emotional monkey brain (limbic system) has taken over and we're making decisions based on the emotions we're feeling in the moment. The monkey brain is ideal for dangerous fight-or-flight situations but counterproductive to helping us make a sales pitch.

The problem we all face is our monkey brain is much stronger and operates five times faster than our human brain. This means we need lots of energy to stay in control of our emotions, especially when we are stressed. When we're a bad CEO, we run out of energy to control our emotions and impulses. The article below outlines three strategies you can use to keep your human brain online and become a better chief energy officer each day.

 Read the article: "How To Become a 'CEO' in Sales."

AUGUST, Day 137: ABCs of Anxiety

According to Dr. Albert Ellis, if you're feeling anxious today, remember your ABCs of anxiety: alarm, belief, coping.[4] Knowing our ABCs help us understand how anxiety works so we can work with it rather than against it.

Feeling *anxious* starts when we experience an *alarm* in our environment such as losing a deal. Next, our brain will evaluate the alarm and develop a *belief* about the observation we just made. From there we *cope* and either react to the alarm in a negative way, which may trigger more alarms, or we respond in a positive way that prevents a downward spiral. Here is an example of how a downward spiral starts:

> *Alarm: Lose a deal you told your manager would close.*
>
> *Belief: My manager is going to be so mad at me.*
>
> *Coping: Procrastinate and think of an excuse.*
>
> *Alarm: Manager asks you about the deal in your one-on-one.*
>
> *Belief: I'm going to lose my job if I tell them the truth.*
>
> *Coping: Lie and tell them you're still working on it.*

Consequence of prolonged downward spiral: losing your job weeks later due to poor performance.

You need to be mindful of this cycle happening on a daily basis. There will always be alarms in sales, which you cannot control, but maintaining a healthy pipeline will allow beliefs to remain hopeful. You also control your coping mechanisms, so be conscious of whether these coping mechanisms are helping or hurting. Our mood follows our behavior, and coping with good habits (filling our pipeline, telling the truth, showing compassion, taking accountability, etc.) can quickly break this ABC cycle. Today, focus on these two areas and put your knowledge of ABCs to good use:

1. What alarms can you control and remove from your environment? Example: Limit social media, spend less time with people who make you upset, leave work early to avoid traffic.
2. When you do encounter an alarm, how can you cope in a healthy way to start building good habits? Example: If you get rejected, practice visualizing a customer who really needs your help, rather than carrying your negative emotions over to the next call. Example: If a buyer is ghosting you, then brainstorm creative ways to reengage them or find a new way into the account through a different prospect.

AUGUST, Day 138: Sales and Masks

Have you ever worn one of those thick rubber Halloween masks? Trying to sell when you're anxious can feel like you're wearing one of those masks all day.

When I was a kid, every time I put one of those masks on I felt like a different person, who was very uncomfortable. I felt hot and overheated. I felt short of breath and couldn't breathe. I felt my mouth dry up and my perception narrow to a point where I could only see what was directly in front of me. All I could hear was my voice in my mask as it echoed around the rubber encasing. This experience of wearing a Halloween mask will sound familiar to those with sales anxiety, who are trying to sell while wearing a mask and can't be their authentic self at work.

Now how good does it feel to take that mask off; when you can be yourself and you can breathe again; when you can see, hear, feel, taste, and smell the world around you; when you can think clearly again and listen to others; when you can perceive opportunities that you have been missing because of your mask? Pretty amazing, right?

Sales leaders, this is one of the most important duties you have: creating a safe place where your team doesn't feel the need to protect themselves by wearing a mask, where they can talk about mental health while being embraced, loved, and encouraged to be who they truly are.

AUGUST, Day 139: Five Dysfunctions of Mental Health

It's interesting how Patrick Lencioni's book *Five Dysfunctions of a Team*,[5] could also be labeled the *Five Dysfunctions of Mental Health*.

1. **Absence of trust:** Your mind, body, and immune system have been evolving over millions of years. If you don't trust that you have the innate tools to respond to stress or setbacks, you'll have a tough time believing that you can manage your anxiety and depression.
2. **Fear of conflict:** If you fear your inner conflict, you'll never be able to release the emotions, experiences, and memories that are causing your mental health to decline.
3. **Lack of commitment:** Maintaining a positive state of well-being requires daily practice of self-care. Being consistent with caring for yourself requires commitment.
4. **Avoidance of accountability:** If you're constantly blaming others and the world around you, then your mental health will always suffer. You must approach the emotions tied to difficult situations.
5. **Inattention to results:** Improvements in mental health are not immediate. If you're not attentive to small changes in progress and improvement as a result of your hard work and practice, it will be hard to stay motivated.

What main mental health "dysfunction" is holding you back? Can you take one small action to start resolving it today?

AUGUST, Day 140: Your Voice Matters

It may not be Mental Health Awareness month, but don't stop. Don't stop sharing, talking, and working to create spaces where vulnerable mental health conversations can take place within sales. Why? Because consistency leads to change, and using your voice matters more than you think.

Since starting Sales Health Alliance, I've posted four or five times a week on LinkedIn. By the three-year mark, this content had been viewed over three million times, liked over 30,000 times and had received almost 10,000 comments. It started conversations about mental health in sales that may have never taken place. I'm sharing these data points with you to show just how much one person's voice can make a difference when they're consistent.

Every post I made had to align with my North Star metric, which was to provide new insight about mental health in sales. That's because mental health stigma is an invisible wall, and the best way through a wall is to hit the same place on the wall over and over again. Over time you learn how to hit that same spot on the wall stronger, harder, and faster; as a result the wall starts to crumble, and you build momentum for change.

As you look around your world today and see companies, products, restaurants, roads and buildings, remember that 95% of everything you see in this world has been built by someone as capable or less capable than you are right now. So why are you playing by their rules? The only difference between you and them is they decided to get into the ring, use their voice, and fight for something they thought the world needed. Be the change you want to see in the world, and get in the ring to fight for it. Tear down the walls that are preventing more inclusivity, diversity, and equality from existing in the communities you care most about.

AUGUST, Day 141: Mindset and Algorithms

Your mindset and a social media algorithm function in very much the same way. Using LinkedIn as an example, every single second thousands of posts are created on the platform by content creators around the world. Obviously it would be impossible for one person to consume all of this content and find relevant content, so LinkedIn created an algorithm. Based on past experiences and previous engagements, the algorithm automatically combs through all this information and instantly creates a feed of content aligned to your interests. This feed shapes your perspective and beliefs about the LinkedIn world.

Our mindset works the same way. Every single second we are receiving over a million bits of information through our senses—sight, touch, hearing, sound, and taste. Our brain can only consciously process a small part of this information at any given second, so much like an algorithm, our mindset uses past experiences, beliefs, and interests to compress, delete, generalize, and distort this information. It creates a "feed" of information that shapes our perspective and beliefs about the world. In either case, it's easy to get stuck operating on autopilot.

Today, if you catch yourself doomscrolling or caught in a negative thought pattern, make a point to be intentional with your algorithm and your mindset. Make sure you're constantly feeding them with new information to break unhelpful patterns and shape a more positive perspective of the world.

AUGUST, Day 142: The Anxiety Cure

The Dalai Lama once said the cure to our anxiety is altruism, and he is correct. Altruism can simply be characterized by selflessness and having concern for the well-being of others.

When you start to get anxious, what happens? It becomes all about *you*, and salespeople start to tell themselves things such as, "I don't have time to update the CRM—it's a waste of my time," "People are going to hate me if I call them out of the blue," "I'm going to miss my target if I can't get this deal to close," "If this economy doesn't rebound, I'm going to lose my job," or "If I lose my job, my family won't be supported." As we begin to spiral downward, these intrusive thoughts become increasingly more personal, and our level of anxiety increases. When this happens, we often respond to this heightened level of anxiety by doing one of three things:

> **Freeze:** We do nothing and crumple under the weight of these thoughts.
>
> **Fight:** More often we work harder . . . and harder . . . and harder . . . until we burn out.
>
> **Flight:** Or we run away from our problems or try to find ways to distract ourselves.

When we're anxious, our emotional brain (limbic system) has taken over, and we are no longer thinking logically because our prefrontal cortex is shutting down. Our emotional brain is taking over because the anxious thoughts running through our head make us believe we are in real danger of being hurt. Without our prefrontal cortex, it becomes nearly impossible to problem-solve.

One of the best ways to prevent this from happening and build resilience to these intrusive thoughts is to listen to the Dalai Lama, embrace altruism, and ensure our mindset toward our daily tasks is primarily focused on helping and serving others. When we keep our mindset focused on helping others, it becomes harder for our emotional brain to take over and get anxious, because *you* are not in the picture. If *you* are not in the picture, then *you* cannot be perceived as in danger and your brain can relax.

If you're feeling anxious about a meeting, calling block, or something you have to do today, pause and stop thinking about yourself. Instead think about the person you're trying to help, the challenges they're facing, and how you can create the best experience for *them*.

AUGUST, Day 143: Action Thinking

"Thoughts are spontaneous, we can't control them, and trying to suppress negative thinking is futile. What we should work at instead is learning to introduce *new* thoughts and treat it like a behavior that we can control."

This was a sentiment shared by Dr. Andrew Huberman in a recent podcast[6] that really resonated with me because it reminded me of the famous quote: "You cannot think your way into a new way of acting, but you can act your way into a new way of thinking." Introducing new thoughts is an *action* we can all take, so how do we do it effectively? Here are some actions you can take to introduce new thoughts:

1. **Gratitude:** Inject new thoughts about people and experiences that you're grateful for. This will help you feel less alone and more connected to people around you.
2. **Focus on small wins:** Inject new thoughts about small progress being made toward bigger goals to help you stay motivated. These can be minor such as putting your shoes on to go for a run.
3. **Reframing:** Inject new thoughts to help you reframe negative experiences in a more positive light. For example, focus on reframing losses as learning experiences.
4. **Acknowledge the process:** Inject new thoughts that acknowledge the struggle, frustration, and anxiety as part of the growth process. This will help you be more compassionate to yourself.
5. **Self-affirmation:** Inject new thoughts from past experiences where you overcame an obstacle that relates to the one currently standing in your way. Reflecting on these experiences will help you build confidence.
6. **Personal development:** Inject new thoughts from external resources such as books and podcasts. These new insights will help you feel more hopeful and resourceful while under pressure.

What *action* are you going to take to inject new thoughts into how you're thinking today?

AUGUST, Day 144: Interview Candidates

What would you do if a candidate shared their mental health struggles during the interview process? Guessing most sales managers would quietly move them into the "Not a good fit" box in their head.

The majority of sales leaders believe that in order to build a successful sales team, you need to hire "A" players. These are salespeople who embody traits such as empathy, confidence, compassion, and authenticity, traits that will help them connect with new buyers and sell at a high level. To find these people, leaders often rely on complicated questions, personality tests, or culture assessments during the interview process, questions and tests that when asked will help sales leaders determine how strong an interviewee is in these areas. Sometimes they work and sometimes they don't, but often a really good candidate can pass these tests with flying colors and then end up struggling as soon as they get into the role. But what if we're getting this hiring process wrong? What if the topic we avoid the most in sales—mental health—is actually the key to finding the best salespeople we need to build our dream sales team?

When you think about it, the best salespeople are the ones who talk openly about mental health. They embody everything a salesperson needs to be successful because talking about mental health requires someone to be confident, vulnerable, authentic, self-aware, empathetic, and willing to trust others. Not only do these traits make them effective at selling, but it helps sales leaders coach and lead effectively. It becomes easy to be transparent and better understand each other, while inspiring others on the team to lead with these core values.

Complicated interview questions and creating in-depth assessments can be important, but if you're a sales leader, try starting the mental health conversation during the interview process. Don't pry the candidate for information, but instead share openly about your experience and the role mental health plays in your team's day-to-day, so they have an opportunity to reciprocate and open up. Only when the masks are off can both the sales leader and candidate answer the most important question they both have: Will I enjoy working with this person on a regular basis?

AUGUST, Day 145: Dark Horses

Are you a Dark Horse? That's the name of a long-term Harvard study of people who have achieved success through individuality.[7]

We all want to be successful in work, in life, and in sales, but oftentimes when we start exploring the idea of success we start with the wrong question and we ask: What is the best way to achieve success? This first question is flawed because it leads us down a path of turning our attention outward. Looking outward is important (i.e. Who do you want to become?), but too often we start overanalyzing what "successful" people in our community are doing and compare ourselves to them. Overanalyzing can blind us to our own strengths and unique qualities that make us different. This is particularly problematic within sales when the sales dashboard has us comparing people 24/7. We obsess over trying to copy and compare ourselves to others and their success. When we fail or come up short, negative thinking swallows us up and our mental health can suffer.

You can combat the negative consequences of spending too much time looking outward by becoming a Dark Horse and supplement "Who do you want to become" with "What is the best way for *me* to achieve success?" This turns your attention inward so you find your personal strengths and what makes you authentic. From there you can focus on personal growth in the areas you care most about, and success then becomes a by-product of your fulfillment, rather than something you're endlessly chasing.

AUGUST, Day 146: Wellness Day Problems

While providing wellness days is a step in the right direction, there are three primary aspects that are not being properly considered by companies.

1. They Are Reactive

Are managers under-skilled? Is there mental health stigma? Are metrics actually achievable? Wellness days will certainly provide temporary relief, but unless the organization is willing to ask the tough questions, core issues will persist and lead to a dependence on reactive strategies. Action item: *Ask, "Why are people burning out in the first place?"*

2. They Assume Knowledge

Wellness days can be highly effective when an individual has a baseline understanding of mental health and knows what their body needs to recover from stress. What percentage of your team has proper stress-management knowledge? I would guess less than 50%, which means most will use the day watching Netflix, drinking beer, or scrolling through social media. Action Item: *Educate your team on the importance of mental health and provide a toolkit.*

3. They Assume Motivation

It takes discipline and effort to actively recover from stress. If someone is lacking purpose within their role, then the chances they will spend a wellness day maximizing recovery for better performance will be low. Getting better at their job just won't feel important. Action Item: *Align work to what intrinsically motivates people so it feels purposeful.*

AUGUST, Day 147: Social Impact

It can sometimes feel pretty meaningless selling SaaS or other technology products, and such feelings can have a direct impact on motivation and resilience. Rather than run another competition or incentive, sales leaders should spend time understanding what societal issues and movements are really important to reps on their team. For example, these might be issues pertaining to racial inequality, climate change, income inequality, mental health, gender inequality, voting rights, health care, food insecurity, or gun violence.

The world is currently going through a period of extreme change, while facing catastrophic threats to the human race. Compared to these societal issues, selling SaaS technology will be perceived as less important. It's also extremely difficult for salespeople to get involved in the issues they care about outside of work hours because many are severely burnt out and overworked.

To resolve this, sales leaders can find ways to empower their team to get involved with the issues they care most about during the hours of nine to five. Winning vacations or prizes such as a night out with the team are fun and important but not all the time. During your next sales contest, start an initiative that will donate X% of each sale they make to the organization of their choice. This will do way more for engagement and productivity than a $100 spiff ever will.

AUGUST, Day 148: Get in Touch

According to a recent Microsoft study, over 40% of people are considering leaving their jobs.[8] One of the main trends sighted as potentially causing this exodus: "Leaders are out of touch with employees and need a wake-up call."

The shift to remote working has been challenging for leaders because many are feeling disconnected from their team. Without the water cooler chats, in-person meetings, and elevator rides, it can be extremely hard for a leader to know how their sales team is doing without the physical cues these micro-interactions provide each day. With more and more data showing that salespeople are experiencing burnout and looking for new jobs, I believe many leaders are anxious and panicking. As a result they are looking for ways to get people back into the office, receive physical cues, assess how their team is doing (without talking to them), and try to control the situation. A better solution: Talk to them.

Here is a simple framework you can use based on Brené Brown's framework for "Hope" in *Dare to Lead*,[9] which we learned about earlier and can help you have more meaningful conversations with your team and connect on a deeper level:

1. **Vision**

    Company visions and individual salesperson visions have changed. A lot of soul searching and rejuggling of priorities has taken place during and after the pandemic. What are the unique visions each salesperson has for themselves over the next one to three years? Who do they want to become, and what priorities do they have? Action item: *Help make the connection between new company visions or priorities and how they align to new visions and priorities of salespeople.*

2. **Path**

    Things are changing rapidly within sales, which means there are several paths a salesperson may be considering to achieve their new vision and priorities. According to the data, most of these paths may involve changing jobs or taking a sabbatical. Can a different path for your salespeople exist within your company? Action item: *Have honest conversations about their career path. Show them how still working for your company will meet their needs, and help them get to where they are trying to go.*

3. **Agency**

Every single person on this planet desires more agency and control of their lives. The job market continues to lean in favor of the job seekers who are demanding these needs be met. Action item: *Sales leaders, find out how you can give your employees more control within their day-to-day life, and help them feel in control of their vision and path. Snuffing out this agency by forcing those who prefer to work from home back into the office is about the worst thing you can possibly do right now.*

AUGUST, Day 149: Delivering Bad News

Stress associated with delivering bad news to a client in sales is very similar to the stress we feel before making a cold call. Rather than keeping our attention focused on what we can control, we get caught up worrying about things we can't control such as assuming our client will be upset upon hearing the news.

To find out what we should do, I reached out to my friend Dr. Bryan who is an ER doctor. As a result of his profession, Dr. Bryan regularly has to deliver bad news, which is way worse than anything we experience within sales. I thought his expertise would be applicable, and this is what he said when I asked him:

"I find when trying to break bad news, there are a few things I focus on. First I try to establish where they are in the process. Are they expecting bad news? Did they consider it to be a possibility? Understanding their expectations is important. Second, I try not to give more information than what is necessary and focus on being as clear as possible. Third, if there is something important to convey and could be given before the bad news, then I try to do that first. After bad news people have a tendency to stop listening and retaining new information. Finally, I always give time and space for silence. People process information and bad news at different speeds. Be patient and hold space for them to share what they are thinking and feeling."

Mic drop, Dr. Bryan. Next time you find yourself in a challenging situation such as telling a client about a product bug or project delay, remember these four steps when drafting up a script to deliver the bad news:

Step 1: Where are they in the sales process? Are they a new client or someone who has been a client for a very long time? Understanding their expectations is important.

Step 2: Share any important information the client needs to hear before delivering the bad news so they can listen and retain it better.

Step 3: Try not to give more information than what is necessary and focus on being as clear as possible. Stick to answering the following questions pertaining to bad news: What happened? Why did it happen? How does it affect them? When will it be resolved? What is the next step? How will you be supporting them?

Step 4: Be patient and hold space for them to share what they are thinking and feeling. Give your client or buyer the opportunity to express how they're feeling and answer any follow-up questions they may have.

AUGUST, Day 150: Stop Making Excuses

Data from RepVue showed an industry leading SaaS sales organization spends roughly $526 per rep/month on their sales tech stack, which is $6,312 per rep, per year.[10] Sales rep anxiety, depression, burnout, and the inability to manage stress can render that entire investment useless.

That's why I'm consistently shocked when I hear comments from sales leaders about mental health and resilience training like: "It's too expensive," "It's not the right time," "Can we make it shorter?" "I'll get to it next quarter," "I have no budget," or "Our reps are too busy."

My sales leader friends, are you kidding me? Your entire sales tech stack depends on having a human being who is well rested, focused, and able to manage stress effectively. That is how they'll maximize the ROI on all of the expensive CRM, video conferencing, cadence, and proposal, technologies you've already invested into.

If you're like most sales leaders today and spending $0 on mental health, resilience, and mindset training but thousands on sales enablement technology, you need to rethink this process and start investing into the "mental game" of sales. Right now you're leaving thousands, if not millions, of dollars on the table due to performance errors that have lost deals because of stress and declining mental health.

AUGUST Endnotes

1. Brown, B. (2019). *Dare to Lead: Brave Work. Tough Conversations. Whole Hearts.* Diversified Publishing.
2. Csikszentmihalyi, M. (2009b). *Flow: The psychology of optimal experience.* HarperCollins eBooks.
3. Muhlfeit, J., and Costi, M. (2017). *The Positive Leader: How energy and happiness fuel top-performing teams.* Pearson.
4. Ellis, A. (1969a). "A cognitive approach to behavior therapy." *International Journal of Psychiatry*, 8: 896–900.
5. Lencioni, P. M. (2013). *The Five Dysfunctions of a Team: A leadership fable.* (1st ed.). Jossey-Bass.
6. Roll, R. "The Neuroscience of Optimal Performance: Dr. Andrew Huberman." *Rich Roll* podcast. March 7, 2022. https://youtu.be/2ekdc6jCu2E.
7. Hough, L. "Follow The Dark Horse." *Harvard Ed Magazine.* August 2019. https://www.gse.harvard.edu/news/ed/19/08/follow-dark-horse.
8. The Work Trend Index. "The Next Great Disruption Is Hybrid Work—Are We Ready?" Microsoft. March 22, 2021. https://www.microsoft.com/en-us/worklab/work-trend-index/hybrid-work?utm_source=morning_brew.
9. Brown, B. (2019). *Dare to Lead: Brave Work. Tough Conversations. Whole Hearts.* Diversified Publishing.
10. RepVue. https://www.repvue.com/.

SEPTEMBER

SEPTEMBER, Day 151: Stop Wasting Time

Sales *truth* bomb of the day: "You can spend a *reasonable* amount of time attending to feelings and fears, or you can squander an *unreasonable* amount of time managing unproductive behaviors."

This quote by Brené Brown and shared in her book *Dare to Lead* will likely punch most sales leaders right in the gut.[1] Sales culture and how teams are managed are structurally broken on so many levels. At the root of this dysfunction is an industry that keeps trying to engineer emotion and vulnerability out of sales as we try to turn people into machines. This is not working, and we're spending an *unreasonable* amount of time managing unproductive behaviors with outdated management strategies that aren't working.

We have to accept the fact that working in sales can be scary, emotional, and vulnerable. Sales is human. Spending a *reasonable* amount of time breaking mental health stigmas in sales and creating a space for vulnerable emotions to be discussed is the most efficient way to achieve consistently high performance in the twenty-first century. If you need help doing this, consider the one-hour sales kickoff I deliver to sales teams at your next upcoming event.

Access the program outline for one-hour sales kickoff.

SEPTEMBER, Day 152: Suicide Prevention

Every year, one week in September is dedicated to suicide prevention. One week is not enough, and suicide prevention needs to be an everyday conversation because did you know someone commits suicide every 40 seconds?[2] By the time you're done reading this page, that's one life. Don't think mental health is a first-world problem? High-income countries have the highest rate of suicide per 100,000 people, and suicide is the second leading cause of death among young people. Not a workplace problem? Mental health and substance abuse cost US businesses between $80 and $100 billion a year.

You might be thinking that these statistics don't matter to you, your team, and your family until they all of a sudden do. If someone close to you has been acting a little different lately, check in on them. Small behavior changes in others are often clues that something bigger is going on. They usually happen when our friends, colleagues, partners, or family members are wrestling with something internally and are having trouble asking for help. Let them know you're thinking about them and how meaningful they are to you. Show them you care and do something nice for them today.

SEPTEMBER, Day 153: Push-Ups and Sales Burnout

We can learn a lot about stress, recovery, and sales burnout by completing this short experiment: Try doing as many push-ups as you can in a row.

For the purpose of explaining why this experiment is relevant to sales burnout, let's assume the absolute maximum number of push-ups you can do is 30 in a row. Your experience will likely look something like this: Push-ups 1 and 2 will probably feel a little boring. During push-ups 3 to 18 you'll start to feel excited, energized, focused, and challenged by your goal. Your body is warming up and starts to adapt to the physical stress the push-ups are adding to your body. Around push-up 20, fatigue will start to set in. Your arms may start to shake, you'll slow down, and your form will start to break down as your body tries to find shortcuts to manage the buildup of stress. But you keep going and squeeze out another 10 push-ups until you totally exhaust your muscles, and your body collapses to the ground.

Now, what would happen to your push-up performance if you waited 10 seconds and tried to do it again? Future push-up performance will depend on your recovery period, which allows your body to off-load stress that was added to your body. The amount of stress your body encountered, the length of your recovery period, and the actions you take during this period of rest will have a direct impact on future performance.

For example, if you waited 10 seconds and tried to replicate 30 push-ups again, you'd likely only be able to produce a fraction of what you did the first time. If you waited a day and during that time you stretched, learned about proper push-up form, and got a massage, you could likely replicate or perform higher than the 30 push-ups you did a day earlier. This is the difference between using good stress (eustress) for growth and bad stress (distress) for diminishing returns.

Creating recovery periods to off-load stress is nonnegotiable if we want to maximize the time we spend in the optimal performance zone, the place when we're feeling energized, focused, and challenged. You'll experience this same curve in performance during a mentally challenging day in sales as you did doing a physically challenging push-up routine. If you're not off-loading stress regularly through self-care activities and attending to what your body needs (sleep, nutrition, exercise), your performance will suffer.

In order to perform our best within sales, we need to think about managing our day like a good personal trainer at the gym. Be mindful of how much stress our mind and body are encountering throughout the day so we can maximize daily recovery periods and prevent burnout.

SEPTEMBER, Day 154: Sales Biases

According to Daniel Kahneman, we have to make a conscious effort to not let our biases distort our perception of the world.[3] Biases are cognitive distortions that warp our thinking and make us perceive more threat and more exposure in our environment. As a result, the alarm bells of sales anxiety ring even louder, making it impossible to perform our best on the task at hand. These are five cognitive distortions affecting salespeople today and something high-performance coach Sascha Heinemann talks about regularly.[4]

1. **All-or-nothing thinking:** You adopt black-and-white thinking. If your performance falls short of perfect, you see yourself as a total failure. Example: "If I don't hit 100% of my target, I'm a total failure."
2. **Overgeneralizing:** If one thing goes wrong, you think that it will all go wrong. Example: "That call didn't go well, so neither will the next one."
3. **Mental filtering:** Of all the things going well, you pick one negative detail out and put all of your attention on it. Example: You have a successful morning building your pipeline but can't seem to get past the angry client email you received.
4. **Overusing "should" statements:** You lead with your personal expectations of how the world should work. When people don't meet these expectations, you get upset and blame yourself or others. Example: "Why is that buyer not responding? I wrote the perfect email. They *should* respond."
5. **Emotional reasoning:** You choose emotions over objective evidence and facts. As a result, you believe the emotions you're feeling are telling the truth of what's actually happening. Example: "I'm so worried I'm going to lose this deal—I just know it's going to happen." (Even though the buyer responded positively in an email a day earlier.)

When we let biases control our mindset, our sales performance and mental health will suffer. Make a list of what events in sales and in your life trigger these biases in yourself. Then brainstorm counterarguments to help you combat their effect.

If these biases don't sound like you, scan here and read about **five more cognitive biases** you need to know about in order to master your anxiety in sales.

SEPTEMBER, Day 155: Types of Sales Stressors

Missing targets, deals falling through, buyers ghosting, and facing rejection are all stressors that salespeople face on a daily basis. Often, however, it's not the event itself that affects our mental health, it's how we perceive them. When we think about stressors we encounter throughout our lives, they typically fall into one of four buckets[5]:

1. **Ambient stressors:** Pollution, noise, pesticides, or things in our environment that are adding stress to our bodies, but we are not consciously aware of them.
2. **Daily hassles stressors:** Getting stuck in traffic, waiting in line, or facing setbacks at work or in our personal lives.
3. **Life-changing stressors:** Losing a family member, losing your job, or even positive events like going to university for the first time or getting married.
4. **Catastrophic stressors:** Climate change, COVID, and any other stressor that creates a high degree of damage in that moment, creates future threats, and are challenging to overcome.

When we start perceiving a deal falling through as a life-changing or catastrophic event, it's a good sign we need to pause and reflect on how we're feeling. When we take good care of ourselves and prioritize our mental health, we increase our chances of perceiving stressors we face in sales in a healthy way. As a daily hassle and setback that we need to overcome.

SEPTEMBER, Day 156: Swing Votes

Research outlined by Dr. Michael Gervais on a recent episode of the *Rich Roll* podcast explains that a company culture is broken down into three different groups.[6] Within sales it looks like this:

1. **Engaged:** One third of the salespeople you work with are fully engaged. They believe in the company mission and purpose, while embracing a shared values system.
2. **Not engaged:** One third of the salespeople you work with are not engaged. They are there for a job and don't really care about the company long term.
3. **Swing votes:** One third of the salespeople you work with are swing votes and are undecided. Some days they are deeply engaged and living the company values, while on other days they are disengaged from them.

The key to building a thriving sales team is to work with the swing vote group and move as many of these people as possible into the engaged group. Same is true when trying to build a more supportive mental health culture, which means if you're a mental health advocate, try following these steps:

Step 1: Find your fellow mental health allies who share your values and beliefs about the importance of mental health in the workplace. These are people who are engaged in the mental health conversation. If you don't know where to start, try sharing a post from Sales Health Alliance in an internal Slack channel and ask people what they think.

Step 2: Work with your allies to address the workplace mental health stigma and the barriers that are affecting your culture. The goal should be to make it as easy as possible for your peers that are on the fence about mental health to feel safe about opening up so they can transition into an ally. There will always be resistance to change, which means finding your allies is the most important part.

SEPTEMBER, Day 157: Fear of Loss

Fear of loss can be a powerful motivator for change and growth. It can also be a powerful motivator for burnout, especially when the fear of loss is about losing your job. The latter is common in sales, and most managers will happily leave the "fear of loss" switch left on because it means their reps will work longer hours for machine-like KPIs to feel "safe."

When sales reps fall behind their target, fear of loss will motivate them to keep pushing at the expense of everything else in their life such as mental and physical health, good habits, boundaries, relationships, and friendships. Fear of loss is so powerful that it can erode the foundational parts of who we are without us being consciously aware of it happening. In a normal world this is inhumane and not sustainable. In a recovering post-pandemic world, this is catastrophic.

Sales leaders, try turning the switch off today. Recognize each rep on your team for their hard work, and remind them their job is safe, even those who may be behind or having a tough month. Providing more safety is always the best gift you can give them.

SEPTEMBER, Day 158: Doing the Dishes

Why do you wash the dishes? This might seem like a really stupid question, but the lesson it teaches might save you from making a really big mistake in your sales career.

When I think about my own answer to this question, I could answer it in three different ways. Depending on which answer I choose, the way I perceive the task will change and will affect how fulfilled I'll feel washing dishes. For example, I wash dishes because:

1. It's a chore and something I have to do (low fulfillment);
2. I want to eat off clean dishes (medium fulfillment);
3. It will make my girlfriend happy and make her day easier (high fulfillment).

Every single day of your life is made up of tasks such as washing dishes, but it's extremely empowering to know that you always get to make a choice on how you perceive them. You can choose to perceive them as boring and undesirable annoyances that you would rather not do, or you can choose to perceive them as meaningful and important tasks that can improve the lives of the people you care most about.

If you're feeling unfulfilled and thinking about quitting your job at a great company, which previously made you very feel happy and fulfilled, pause and complete the following steps:

1. Write *all* your work tasks on a piece of paper.
2. Write your reasons for doing each one.
3. Reframe each reason to focus on serving others.

This is a process called job crafting that was created by Yale Professor Amy Wrzesniewski.[7] It's proven to boost levels of fulfillment at work and an exercise I use every time I feel like giving up. The actual task we're working on rarely matters. It's the meaning we tie to them that is most important.

PS. Don't forget about the importance of mental health. This exercise is much harder and less effective when you're feeling anxious and overwhelmed. If you're feeling this way currently, then prioritize some self-care this evening, get a good night's sleep, and try doing it in the morning when you're well rested.

SEPTEMBER, Day 159: Control Your Information

When I watched the *Social Dilemma* on Netflix, it got me thinking about control. As you scroll through information on LinkedIn, Instagram, or Facebook, who do you think is in more control? You or the social media algorithm?

It's crazy to think how much information we consume on a daily basis that is not intentionally chosen by ourselves. What we learn and how we learn is often fed to us by algorithms built to learn everything about us. These algorithms are not built with good intentions to improve our lives but built to learn how to monetize the most valuable resource we have—our time. Time that could be spent taking better care of ourselves, listening to those close to us, and deciding what we believe is important in our lives; decisions that are freely chosen and not fed to us by robots.

I'm trying to be more intentional with my time and the information I consume on a daily basis. One way I've successfully done this is through newsletters from content creators and experts I respect. The caveat is I signed up for these newsletters under a new email account. That way this email inbox becomes my own personal newspaper with information I've chosen and from people with opinions I intentionally want to listen to.

If you have been enjoying this book on mental health in sales and want to add my free newsletter to your list, you can sign up for my free newsletter by scanning here.

SEPTEMBER, Day 160: Bad Outcomes of Success

We have a bias to equate the quality of our decisions to the quality of the outcomes. Sales teams are *obsessed* with outcomes, and if someone hits their sales target (outcome), we automatically assume that they were making "smart" decisions, which is not always true. The problem with this bias is that the margin between success and failure is usually razor thin, and the difference between success and failure can come down to the final days of the month.

Only when someone fails do we ask, "What's wrong?" When someone is hitting their sales target consistently, they are perceived as a top performer and a person who must have made good decisions to achieve this outcome. But this isn't always the case, because often top performers in sales are the ones constantly making bad decisions that are affecting their mental health. They are the ones with the money and the resources to regularly access excess sex, drugs, and alcohol in their personal lives, activities that will accelerate them toward catastrophic burnout, and no one will notice until it's too late. Why? Because they've been hitting target and we assume everything must be fine.

I know this because it happened to me early on in my career. Don't just assume a top performer is okay. Check in on them, especially after they've had a great month or quarter.

SEPTEMBER, Day 161: The Pre-call Ritual

Why do you think all great athletes have a structured pregame ritual they follow before every game or competition? It's because they all know that their mind is the precursor for performing their craft. If their mind is unfocused, anxious, or overwhelmed by the moment, then they'll have a tough time performing their craft at a high level, especially while under extreme pressure from others and time constraints.

Similar time constraints and pressure also exist within sales. We have a limited amount of time to impress a new buyer or prospect, which means we need to make every second count. That's why I've put together a seven-step process to help you and your fellow salespeople get your mind right before your next sales pitch. You can use this seven-step process as a pregame warm-up to a sales call or meeting that will ensure you're laser focused and prepared to perform your best.

It's only when we're operating in the present that we'll be able to deliver a compelling message to our buyers.

Scan here for the free seven-step process to maximize your pre-call or -meeting ritual.

SEPTEMBER, Day 162: Needs vs Wants

There is a paradox that exists when we start trying to prioritize better mental health in our lives, which is what we need is not always what we want. This statement becomes especially true for those of us working within a stressful sales environment and an increasingly digital world filled with distractions. In these environments, our needs often become misaligned with our wants, making it hard to consistently prioritize our mental health.

If you wake up Monday morning after experiencing a terrible sleep, you're likely to say to yourself: "I need to go to sleep early tonight" because your desire to want to sleep at that moment is high. *Both your needs and wants are aligned.* Since you just woke up, there are few distractions, making your decision to want to fulfill your need later that day crystal clear, and the choice is easy. As the day progresses this choice becomes less easy and more unclear. We are presented with an avalanche of choices, distractions, and pressure, which break our alignment and knock us off balance:

"I *need* to take a break, but I *want* to respond to that email."
"I *need* to prioritize mental health with my team, but I *want* them to make more calls."
"I *need* to go for lunch, but I *want* to prepare for my meeting."
"I *need* to go to sleep early, but I *want* to keep watching Netflix."

What we need no longer becomes what we want, and your logical needs for better long-term health are being overpowered by your emotional needs of the moment, hence the paradox.

We can break this paradox by bringing more awareness to aligning our needs and wants throughout the day. On a piece of paper complete this exercise and write out: "I NEED TO prioritize self-care today, because I WANT TO feel less anxious, stressed, tired, burnout, etc. (insert whatever emotion you no longer wish to feel)." Stick this paper somewhere visible so you will see it multiple times throughout the day, and read it out loud when you see it.

By writing this statement out on a piece of paper you connect the logical need of self-care with the emotional want and desire you have to no longer feel a certain way. In doing so you are aligning the two parts of your brain that are responsible for making decisions and making yourself less susceptible to conflicting emotional choices that arise throughout the day that affect your mental health.

SEPTEMBER, Day 163: Sales Needs Emotion

When was the last time you persevered through stress, discomfort, and pain for something that was meaningless to you? Probably never. We usually quit, give up, or invest minimal effort on tasks that *feel* meaningless. This is why meaningful work is so important to resilience and one of the primary reasons why the sales industry is getting peak performance so wrong. We keep trying to engineer emotion out of our sales teams, when instead, we should be doing the exact opposite.

Meaningful work is rooted in emotion, and our work needs to matter to us. We need to care about our company's vision, our customers, and believe the products we're selling improve the lives of others. Far too often these aspects that create meaning get lost behind the stress of machine-like metrics and rejection that salespeople face each day. To make matters worse, we're scared to talk about how we're feeling with others and fear being labeled "lazy" or the "weak link" on the team.

When working in sales starts to feel meaningless and motivation dries up, asking yourself these five questions can make all the difference in rediscovering your core motivator:

1. When you first joined your company, why were you excited to work there? (X)
2. Why was X important to you at that time?
3. Is X still really important to you today or has X changed?
4. What's currently getting in the way of X?
5. If X has changed, what needs to change in your daily routine or working environment to better align with what matters most to you about work?

I've always found answering these five questions particularly insightful whenever I'm having trouble with motivation. I normally walk away with some key insights around things that are blocking my motivation or new aspects of my life that have become important that I need to do a better job integrating into work. Even better, I have a clear understanding of what I need from peers and managers to help me shape an environment where I perform my best. Hopefully the exercise will yield similar results for you.

SEPTEMBER, Day 164: Drinking on the Job

A major negative consequence of remote work was brought to my attention recently, and I don't think many sales leaders are currently aware of it: Junior sales reps are drinking on the job, while at home to "perform better." I learned about this from a post that was shared with me from r/sales on Reddit and read:

> "I can feel a problem developing. I've been working as a BDR (cold calls) since March. I'm doing pretty good at it but I notice myself drinking more to do a better job. I normally drink just for fun, but now I drink every day and now I'm drinking to perform better. I'm scared. Anybody else use drugs/alcohol to do better at your remote sales job?"

Thankfully the vast majority of the comments expressed concern, condoned the behavior, and provided helpful feedback, but what stuck with me was how easy remote working has made it to drink on the job. It also made me realize I easily could have been that rep. Fresh out of a heavy party culture in university, the first sales company I worked for in 2011 had intense metrics of making 200 dials a day and achieving two and a half hours of talk time. Rejection, pressure, and stress were unrelenting. The company also had a culture that regularly involved lunchtime beers. Like the Sirens in the *Odyssey* that lured sailors to their destruction with their irresistible singing, these lunchtime beers lured me and other junior reps into thinking they helped us sell better. We felt more confident on calls, stress temporarily felt more manageable, and the difficult emotions tied to rejection didn't hurt as bad. But here is the problem with using drugs and alcohol to amplify performance:

- Your brain starts to believe it can't do X without Y;
- You build a tolerance and keep needing more;
- Daytime drinks lead to nighttime drinks;
- Sleep, motivation, health, and performance are all affected.

But the worst part is drugs and alcohol become your default coping mechanism. Drinking and/or doing drugs to cope with work stress becomes a bad habit you use to cope with stress in other areas of your life outside of work. Because your mental health, well-being, and performance are being negatively affected, mistakes get made, relationships get damaged, stressors build up, and downward spirals accelerate. Bad habits become addictions, and the race to the bottom begins.

So to all the brand-new sales folks out there, don't get tricked into thinking alcohol helps you perform better. It doesn't. What you need is a proper toolkit to help you manage and protect your mental health so you can navigate these unique sales stressors in a healthy way. Remember to keep checking Sales Health Alliance because there are over 100 free resources to help you get started.

SEPTEMBER, Day 165: Playing the Long Game

Why do you think general managers take pitchers out of a baseball game when they're on pace to pitch a perfect game? They're playing the long game and protecting their players. General managers have learned that one of the most important metrics to prioritize for long-term pitcher health is "pitch count" over anything else. This comes ahead of short-term performance such as winning the game or pitching a no hitter. They know when pitch count gets too high, the risk of injury and the pitcher blowing out their arm is no longer worth the short-term gains in performance. You know who is usually most upset by this? The pitcher who wants to keep playing.

Whether it's the MLB, NBA, or NHL, medical teams have been empowered to make data-driven decisions to sit out players, even when the coaches want to play them or the players feel fine. As former NBA player Richard Jefferson said recently, "It's no longer a badge of honor to play 82 games in a season. It's about how do we stay healthy and preserve player health for the long run, to justify the money the team has invested into the player."

In an industry that is riddled with burnout, the sales community has a lot to learn from the advances in burnout and injury prevention being made in sports. Sales leaders need to start playing the long game, and they need to start using health data to inform decisions. They also need to sit out sellers who are skipping vacations, working through weekends, and putting their own mental health at risk, even if they're about to "pitch a perfect year" and hit target four consecutive quarters in a row. Top sellers like top athletes want to keep competing—no matter what. But that's not always what's best for them or the sales organization in the long term.

So how do we get there? One important starting point would be providing sellers with more guaranteed money in terms of base compensation, rather than the 50/50 carrot-and-stick performance model that prevents the long game from ever being considered or played. When salespeople have access to more guaranteed money, it incentivizes sales organizations to prioritize the long-term health of their people.

SEPTEMBER, Day 166: No One Is Wearing Shoes!

This is a short story you've likely heard before, to illustrate the massive opportunity organizations have within workplace mental health and sales.

Many years ago, a company sent two salespeople to two small towns in an under developed region of the world to evaluate the market opportunity for their burgeoning shoe business. During their first two weeks, each salesperson explored their territory and spoke to potential customers. After their territory planning and evaluation were completed, each salesperson sent a telegram back home explaining the opportunity that their company had in this new market. The first salesperson sent this message: "No opportunity here. No one here wears any shoes!" The second salesperson sent this message instead: "HUGE opportunity for growth. No one is wearing any shoes yet!"

I love this adage because it eloquently describes the importance of perspective and the influence it has on how we experience the world around us. Two people in almost the exact same situation or environment can have two wildly different beliefs, attitudes, and opinions based on their mindset and what they perceive. Regardless of whether we're objectively right or wrong, we all have a very narrow perspective into the world around us. If you lead with a belief that mental health is not a priority within sales, then you're going to miss the *huge* opportunity right in front of you, which is: there are hardly any salespeople wearing "shoes" (i.e. prioritizing mental health) today. Be like the second salesperson in the adage and get an edge in performance by being first to develop a mental health and resilience toolkit for yourself.

SEPTEMBER, Day 167: High Strain Activities

Public speaking still makes me incredibly nervous and uncomfortable. Speaking engagements are *high* mental strain activities that need *high* mental recoveries for me to perform my best. That's why I block time after each podcast or presentation I do to help my mind rest and recover. Without it, I know my performance on future tasks won't be as good, and I run the risk of burning myself out.

You need to build awareness around the sales activities and experiences that make you most uncomfortable. For example, if cold-calling makes you really anxious, make sure you have a 20-minute recovery period after your call block before jumping into a demo with a client. If rejection really affects you, make sure you pause, inhale for four seconds, and exhale for six seconds (repeat 10 times), so you can help reset your stress response before moving forward.

Finding that balance between mental strain and mental recovery will help you perform your best and allow you to use stress to your advantage and grow. Performing this consistently over time will help you manage the stress associated with developing a weaknesses or skill into a strength without burning out.

SEPTEMBER, Day 168: Stop Aiming for Perfect

Do *not* try to be perfect while working in sales. With sales targets constantly on the rise, perfectionists are usually the ones that burn out the fastest. I know this because I was one. "Being perfect" is a desired state that will never be reached, and your chase for perfection will only result in one of these two undesirable outcomes:

1. **Your Ego Will Explode**

   You will perceive yourself as being perfect, which will turn you into an arrogant a**hole that no one wants to be around. The opposite of perfect. Even worse, when you think you're perfect, you believe there is nothing left to learn, and your lack of humility will put you in a race to the bottom.

2. **Your Ego Will Implode**

   You will be crushed by the weight of your negative self-talk that is constantly telling you that you'll never be good enough or worthy of love. Sales is hard, and if you hope to succeed, your best friend needs to be *you*.

Go easy on yourself today, and if that call, meeting, or email wasn't "perfect," then that's okay. What did you learn, and how can you implement what you learned on your next call, meeting, or email? Learn it, implement it, and then move on.

SEPTEMBER, Day 169: Intermittent Fasting

At some point, you've likely heard about the benefits of intermittent fasting, but maybe you're not sure how it relates to sales performance. Depending on your goals, you also may not be fasting in an optimal way.

If you do a Google search for the "benefits of intermittent fasting," you'll find thousands of articles and research-backed data points that show you intermittent fasting has proven to help people lose weight, build muscle, enhance heart health, repair cells, and lower inflammation. The benefit I'm most interested in achieving through fasting is boosting cognitive focus. Working in sales and running a business is primarily a mental game. This means I'm always looking for ways to improve my focus and speed up my learning.

Intermittent fasting is usually defined as fasting for ~16 hours during a 24-hour period. For me this usually means not eating between 7 p.m. to 11 a.m. (16 hours) and then consuming all my meals between 11 a.m. and 7 p.m. (8 hours). The reason intermittent fasting helps boost cognitive focus is largely due to the role it plays in helping your body release additional cortisol. As our blood sugar falls (from fasting/not eating) cortisol and adrenaline are released into the body. This survival system was designed to get us moving and find food so we don't starve.

When we finally eat food, our body releases insulin, which blunts the effect of cortisol and adrenaline, which allows them to return to normal levels. When our blood sugar drops and we get hungry again (aka hunger stress), the system restarts.

The cool part is cortisol also plays an extremely important role in learning and focus. The media typically describes cortisol as the "evil stress hormone" we should avoid. In reality, we can use intermittent fasting to slightly elevate our cortisol levels to improve our performance.

Too much cortisol = bad stress, anxiety, and poor performance.

Slightly elevated cortisol = good stress, focus, and optimal performance.

It's finding the right balance of cortisol where salespeople usually get intermittent fasting wrong because they don't adapt their eating habits to their high-stress sales environment.

To learn how to do this effectively and integrate the benefits of intermittent fasting into your day, scan below and scroll to the middle of the article as I outline how to best use it as a tool for better sales performance.

SEPTEMBER, Day 170: Input-Focused Mindset

Getting blindsided by an unexpected testicular cancer diagnosis like I did in 2018 had striking similarities to the anxiety felt after losing a deal in sales that I spent months working on.

The weeks after my diagnosis were ripe with uncertainty, anxiety, and fear as I went through the next steps with my doctor. For weeks I had to tussle with the same intrusive thoughts that kept trying to take over. "What if the surgery doesn't work?" "What if the cancer had spread?" or "What if I don't make it through this?" These thoughts reminded me a lot of the ones I would face regularly in sales such as "What if that deal doesn't close?" "What if I miss my target?" or "What if I lose my job?"

These intrusive thoughts happen when we become too focused on an outcome we want to achieve. This is an *outcome-focused mindset* that fuels anxiety. Sure I wanted to recover from cancer (outcome), but I couldn't really control that. Sure you may want that big deal to close (outcome), but there will always be factors outside our control. Asking yourself this famous self-help question will help refocus your mindset and help you detach from the outcomes: "What would you do if you knew that you might very well fail?"

I love this question because it forces you to think about uncomfortable worst-case scenarios and find positive actions you can still take. For example, if I knew I was going to be entering a long battle with cancer, I would want to be entering that battle in the best possible shape and with the support of my family and friends. So I actioned more exercise, nutrition, and wellness in the weeks leading up to surgery, while involving those close to me in the process.

This same approach also works in sales. If you knew you would eventually lose that big deal you were working on, what would you do? You would likely start prospecting to find net new business. You would double down on your practice, your mental game, and execute extra daily calls and emails to ensure you had a full pipeline regardless. These are the actions you can always control in sales, like a basketball player who takes thousands of shots each day because they know this type of input leads to better outcomes in the future.

As Ozan Varol stated in his book *Think Like a Rocket Scientist*[8]: "By taking pressure off the outcome you get better at your craft. Success becomes a consequence, not the goal." When you adopt an input-focused mindset that prioritizes daily action, you remove uncertainty from the equation. As a result you don't give your sales anxiety anything to feed off, and you suffocate intrusive thoughts before they can take over.

SEPTEMBER Endnotes

1. Brown, B. (2019). *Dare to Lead: Brave Work. Tough Conversations. Whole Hearts*. Diversified Publishing.
2. "Suicide: one person dies every 40 seconds." World Health Organization. September 9, 2019. https://www.who.int/news/item/09-09-2019-suicide-one-person-dies-every-40-seconds.
3. Kahneman, D. (2012). *Thinking, Fast and Slow*. Kimyoungsa/Tsai Fong Books.
4. Sascha Heinemann. https://saschaheinemann.com/
5. Guski, R. "Environmental Stress and Health." *International Encyclopedia of the Social & Behavioral Sciences*, 2001.
6. Roll, R. "Dr. Michael Gervais Is the Sensei of Human Performance." *Rich Roll* podcast. October 5, 2020. https://youtu.be/yXmOHP5sBxs.
7. Dutton, A. J. Wrzesniewski. *What Job Crafting Looks Like*. Harvard Business Review. March 12, 2020. https://hbr.org/2020/03/what-job-crafting-looks-like.
8. Varol, O. (2021). *Think like a rocket scientist: Simple strategies for giant leaps in work and life*. W H Allen.

OCTOBER

OCTOBER, Day 171: You Don't Need Years of Experience

I'm constantly amazed by the courage of younger sales reps today, who are helping to move the mental health in sales conversation forward in a big way. One of those reps was a rep named Anthony who had recently graduated from college and was six months into an outbound sales role at a high-growth SaaS company.

When Anthony and I connected over the phone, his comments filled me with immense joy as he went on to say: "I read in your book about companies needing to provide sales reps with quota relief when they go on vacation. It really resonated with me because it feels impossible to take time off when quota and metrics don't factor in time off. I brought it up with my sales leaders and my company has now implemented quota relief for sales reps going on vacation!"

I was truly blown away when I heard this because:

1. It took me about seven years to start talking about mental health in sales, not six months.
2. I never would have had the courage to bring this type of initiative up with my sales leadership team at that point in my career.

So thank you for being an inspiration, Anthony. Thank you for showing others you don't need years of experience and it's possible to use your voice for effective change around mental health within sales organizations.

OCTOBER, Day 172: Starting the Conversation

"I want to start talking about my mental health at work and with my manager, but I'm not sure if I can trust them—What should I do?" I get asked this question regularly on LinkedIn or in private conversations with sales reps, and here is my suggestion.

It's very likely that you're not the only one feeling this way. Your teammates and manager are probably struggling, and they also don't know how to approach the topic in the workplace. I always suggest you start small and run an experiment with your team.

At the next team meeting, bring a recent article you've read on mental health that has data from a credible source. Feel free to use any of the articles from this book or from the Sales Health Alliance website. Then simply ask the group: "I was reading an article on workplace mental health that said X . . . I was curious if anyone on the team would be open to brainstorming ideas on how we can make this better?"

Taking this approach will give you an opportunity to read the room and find your allies. You'll likely start a good conversation, or in my experience, people will approach you after looking to get involved. Some team action following the team meeting might be (1) daily meditation, (2) reading this book together, (3) going to the gym at lunch, and (4) starting a "failure Friday's" meeting, where the team meets to discuss and normalize their biggest fails of the week. Start small and build rapport with the team until you feel safe sharing the heavier stuff.

OCTOBER, Day 173: No Brakes

How would you describe driving a car without brakes? Probably using words like dangerous, out of control, risky, unsafe for others, scary, inefficient, questionable, using poor judgment, and a mistake overall. The decision is pretty clear, none of us would get into a car without brakes. But a very similar situation is happening every single day in sales. Millions of salespeople are showing up every single day and working without "brakes," which is why many of us would describe our work life using the exact same words.

One of the foundations for improving mental health and resilience at an individual level is learning how to balance our "emotional gas pedal" and "logical brake pedal." Our gas pedal is controlled by a region of the brain called the limbic system, which is responsible for our emotions. Our brake pedal is controlled by our prefrontal cortex, which is responsible for executive functions such as planning, logic, and creativity. When both of these systems are balanced, we can "work within our speed limit" and feel calm, in control, motivated, make good decisions, and perform at a high level. Unfortunately, when we become fatigued, anxious, overworked, overwhelmed, depressed, burnt out, etc., and don't have a toolkit to manage our stress levels, our brake pedal starts to go offline. We're "driving" (aka working) without brakes.

So what would you do if you were driving a car with no brakes? Well, you would probably slow down, ask someone knowledgeable for help, identify why your brakes broke, learn how to fix them, and get back to driving at the speed limit. These exact same strategies apply to your mental health and when your emotions are speeding out of control.

OCTOBER, Day 174: What Is Empathy Really?

"Empathetic" is the word used to describe how salespeople should approach their prospects and relate to the challenges they are facing. But there is a lot of fake empathy going around, so let's clear this up.

To be truly empathetic you must combine two types of empathy: cognitive and affective empathy. Cognitive empathy is the ability to understand another person's perspective and see things from their point of view. When you're using cognitive empathy muscles, you would agree with statements such as:

"I can identify challenges my buyer may be facing before they tell me."
"I know when a buyer is upset before they say why."
"I can easily see things from a buyer's perspective."

Most empathy in sales stops here, but this is not being empathetic. Exploiting buyer weaknesses to benefit our own selling is just manipulative. Enter affective empathy, which is the ability to feel what a buyer is feeling and live their emotional experience. When you're using affective empathy muscles, you would agree with statements such as:

"I feel the buyer's pain when they tell me about X challenge."
"I would feel bad if my product let the buyer down after purchase."
"I would be upset if the buyer bought the wrong solution."

If you're not feeling buyer emotions, you're not being empathetic. You need to understand *and* feel your buyer's emotions to show true empathy in sales. Before your next important call or meeting, try to imagine a day in the life of your buyer, and *feel* their anguish. This will help you align on an emotional level. The best part is sellers get to strengthen their empathy muscles on calls with clients every day, which means they'll be in good shape to support colleagues, friends, and family during times of need.

OCTOBER, Day 175: 30 Days of Sweat

You know that sluggish feeling you get after a tough month or feeling stuck in a rut? Here is your remedy: Start a "30 Days of Sweat Challenge" with your friends, family, and/or work teams.

What is that, you ask? It's very simple. All you need to do is sweat once a day for the next 30 days, that's it. You can run stairs in your building, dance to your favorite song, chase your kids around the house, do some jumping jacks, go for a run, or do some push-ups. It doesn't matter what activity you choose, you just have to *sweat* once per day.

Often we have a tendency to overcomplicate and overthink exercise. We think it's going to be expensive, requires an expert to teach us, and needs to be done at a certain time each day. As a result, we find excuses and miss out on all of the benefits exercise has to offer. Exercise releases endorphins and various other neurotransmitters, which helps improve mental clarity, self-esteem, sleep, and the ability to handle stress. It's essentially a miracle cure for better mental health and primes our brain to perform its best each day.

So don't overthink it. Make a list of three or four activities you really enjoy doing, and brainstorm how you can implement more movement into these activities so you sweat while doing them. For example, riding an exercise bike or running on a treadmill, while watching TV, reading a book, or listening to a podcast. Then start a "30 Days of Sweat" Slack channel with your work colleagues or group chat with your family. Post your updates and share videos to help keep everyone accountable and motivated. Kudos to my favorite YouTube channel Yes Theory for inspiring this challenge.

OCTOBER, Day 176: Ryan Reynolds

In 2011, Ryan Reynolds was the laughingstock of Hollywood after starring as Green Lantern in one of the worst superhero movies of all time. In 2022, he was presented with the Governor's General Performing Arts Award. For my non-Canadian friends, this is one of the most prestigious awards a Canadian actor can win.

I can only imagine what he was thinking and feeling after the critics were tearing apart his portrayal of Green Lantern. He probably wanted to give up. He probably wanted to hide. And he probably thought he missed his big break. But instead he kept going, honed his craft, diversified his brand, and focused on serving communities. He also did what all Canadians try to do in the face of adversity and kept being kind to others.

Today, if you feel like you're not living up to your full potential or struggling to succeed in sales, then this may just be your Green Lantern. Zoom out and remember that a lot can change in 10 years. What you're experiencing right now is temporary. When you're disciplined in your craft and remain focused on serving the people and communities around you, eventually the tide turns in your favor. Thanks for the inspiration today, Deadpool!

OCTOBER, Day 177: RATT

When you're making progress toward learning something new, it's very easy to keep thoughts of self-doubt quiet. My process for doing this consistently is using the acronym RATT.

"R" - Read It

Reading actual books is a skill I've prioritized over the last few years that has provided me with tremendous growth. In a world filled with distractions and surface-level three-minute blog posts, we've become obsessed with learning very little about *a lot* of different topics. Developing your attention span and discipline to actually sit down and slowly read a book will allow your brain to stack complex learnings on top of each other.

"A" - Apply It

Whatever you're reading, highlight and take notes so you can apply it to something you're passionate about. For me I'm always trying to connect it back to sales mental health (X). When we're learning something new and constantly thinking about, "How does this apply to X?" it forces your brain to build new connections and create context so the information is more memorable.

"T" - Try It

Reading something in a book is great, but until you try it, you'll never know if it works for you and your environment. Experimenting with something new helps your brain integrate this new information into its current way of thinking and acting, which again helps improve retention.

"T" - Teach It

Teaching others is one of the best ways to learn because it forces you to consider multiple perspectives. Write a post on LinkedIn, create a blog, or start a company. Sharing and teaching will also provide you with consistent feedback on how much you've learned and the progress you have made, to help fuel more learning going forward.

OCTOBER, Day 178: Working for Workers Act

I'm excited to see the Ontario government in Canada stepping into the ring to tackle workplace burnout with new legislation. It's called the "Working for Workers Act." It was passed recently and businesses with 25 or more people will now have to create a written policy that outlines employee rights as it pertains to disconnecting from work. These policies would include rights around:

- Responding to messages after hours;
- Responding to messages on vacation;
- Proper vacation planning;
- What apps can be on personal phones.

This is a big deal because legislation around topics like this raises the bar for companies and reduces the stigma employees experience while talking about burnout internally. It normalizes the conversation and holds company cultures accountable to creating more work-life balance.

Imagine going into a job interview for a new sales role and asking: "What internal policies did your company create in response to the Working for Workers Act?" Easy, simple, clear, and no fear. These policies have existed for years in forward-thinking European companies, and it's exciting to see North American legislation starting to prioritize this topic.

OCTOBER, Day 179: Stop Comparing

I'm sure many of us have had this very human thought at some point during our sales careers: "At least I'm not doing as bad as . . . (insert person you're doing better than)."

We as humans love to compare ourselves to the people around us. We have a primal drive that is connected to desiring more status because having a higher status yields many survival benefits in our global community. When someone is worse off than we are, it can make us feel better and can make us feel safe. But why are we feeling unsafe in the first place? Why are we taking pleasure from others who are struggling?

When we start comparing ourselves to others, it's a sign we need to turn inward and explore the hidden messages our emotions are sending so we can find the root of our insecurity. Often, comparing ourselves to others is a coping mechanism that we use to help us repair our own ego and self-esteem, an action that helps mask the fear, envy, jealousy, uncertainty, or self-doubt we're experiencing in our own mind. Though we may feel a little better temporarily, it does nothing but rob us of our long-term happiness and can often backfire in a world with carefully curated social media feeds.

That being said, there are benefits to looking outward occasionally, with one caveat. The most successful people in life aren't comparing themselves to the people behind them, because they are too focused on learning from those who are ahead of them.

OCTOBER, Day 180: Your "Spidey-Sense"

One of the best ways to improve your mental health is to change your relationship with anxiety. Anxiety is your "spidey sense" (yes—I'm a huge superhero nerd), and you need to work with it rather than against it.

Our body and mind love control. When you feel in control of your environment, relationships, and ability to act, your brain thinks: "I'm safe, and I cannot get hurt." This is our comfort zone, and when we're in our comfort zone our brain can relax because it has achieved its primary purpose of protecting us from danger. The problem is this primary objective conflicts with another extremely important objective we all have, which is to live a meaningful life without regrets. Achieving this goal requires us to venture out of our comfort zone and seek out challenging experiences that allow us to grow. We have to put ourselves in vulnerable positions that make us feel temporarily out of control and unsafe.

Personal growth, discomfort, and living a meaningful life are all connected, which means our spidey sense and anxiety goes off like an alarm when we seek them out. Most of us respond by avoiding these situations and jump away from them, but the key to working with your anxiety is jumping toward them. We need to treat these as special moments in life that signal alarms for *growth* instead of alarms for *danger*. When they go off, don't panic; it means your anxiety has found a meaningful experience that will help you learn and expand your comfort zone.

To help rewire our natural instinct to avoid new experiences that make us uncomfortable, I've found success in asking myself one question when I feel myself wanting to say, "No, thanks" to new opportunity: "Am I wanting to say no to this experience because I'm genuinely not interested in it, or am I wanting to say no because this experience makes me scared and uncomfortable?" If it's the latter, I label it as anxiety and jump toward it.

OCTOBER, Day 181: More Sleep = More Sales

I stumbled across this amazing research done by Jeff Kahn and his team at Rise Science that found more sleep leads to more sales.

As part of their research, they did an eight-month controlled trial with a global sales force at a Fortune 500 company.[1] What they uncovered was sellers using Rise to improve their sleep increased monthly revenue by 14% over their peers not using Rise, and sellers who improved their sleep debt (those deficient in sleep) to seven hours increased outbound activity by 50%. This is promising data to help further the discussion that sales organizations are measuring their pipeline in the wrong way.

Calls made, emails sent, meetings booked, and various other sales KPIs are *not* input metrics, they are output metrics. The *real* input metrics revolve around sales rep well-being and mental health, metrics such as are they getting enough sleep? Eating right? Are they feeling anxious, depressed, or experiencing burnout? What's their level of self-esteem? Also, when they encounter a stressful experience within sales such as a deal falling through or missing a target, do they have the right mindset, perspective, and daily habits to respond to these stressors in a mentally healthy way?

The research above shows what happens when we improve just *one* metric. Just think what would happen to sales performance if we made a consistent effort to improve mental health as a whole through proper measurement and support.

OCTOBER, Day 182: "I'm a Failure"

It can be very easy to start thinking, "I am a failure," and a thought like this can paralyze us in sales. Believing we're a failure tends to make the body sluggish, the brain fogs over, and we have aches and pains for no reason. We often become easily irritated by those around us, and we feel totally helpless.

To break this cycle you have to remember that "I am a failure" is very different from "I have failed." "I am a failure" is personal and an identity shift. "I have failed" is the act of failing. It is objective and something you can learn from. When a salesperson gets hung up on, they have failed at building rapport and delivering a compelling message. They are not a failure and can learn to improve their pitch. When a founder has to lay off all their staff, they have failed at keeping their employees employed during a difficult time. They are not a failure and can learn how to better manage major economic events affecting their business. When a spouse snaps at their significant other, in that moment they have failed at being a supportive partner. They are not a failure and can learn to improve their patience and communication.

If you catch yourself thinking, "I am a failure" today, pause and create space between your identity and the experience of failure itself. Label the action you failed at completing and reflect on what you can learn from this moment to keep moving forward.

OCTOBER, Day 183: Seasonal Changes

For those of us living in the northern parts of the northern hemisphere, it's extremely important to be aware of your habits and boundaries right now. Bad habits *love* to form and chip away at our boundaries as the darker and colder days begin, something I've certainly been guilty of letting happen in recent years.

Normally I get up each morning at 7:15 a.m., but when boundaries are secretly being eroded by seasonal changes, I lounge in my darker bedroom and under the warm covers until about 7:45 a.m. My phone screen time also jumps up significantly. It usually hovers around 1–1.5 hours per day, and during these times it averages closer to three hours per day. As a result of these minor changes I start to feel constrained. I have less time each day to complete meaningful tasks and do the things that make me happy.

If you've been feeling a similar way and notice this happening to you, here is a checklist of what you can do to get yourself back on track:

- Check your screen time;
- Delete apps stealing your time;
- Audit your routine—what changed?
- Get outside for ~15 min. each morning;
- Fuel up with a big salad at lunch;
- Do one thing that brings you joy each day;
- Reinforce boundaries (no work emails past 5:00, no phone 1 hr. before bed, no phone in bed).

Us northerners don't get the benefit of warm and sunny weather to help keep the serotonin flowing 365 days a year. We need to be the driver of our mental health, rather than a passenger that's more susceptible to seasonal change.

OCTOBER, Day 184: Maybe They

Are you holding onto anger toward someone in your life? You can help release this uncomfortable emotion with two simple words: "Maybe they . . ." When someone does something hurtful that upsets you such as:

Doesn't respond;

Cuts you off;

Isn't on time;

Invades boundaries;

Yells and shouts;

Doesn't tell the truth;

Forgets;

Reveals a secret.

It's easy to forget that in those moments, that stranger on the street, colleague in your office, friend at dinner, or family member at home is likely just trying their best. It's easy to want to use your anger to seek revenge for how you're feeling by yelling, punching, and retaliating back. But does it help? Rarely.

Holding onto anger, blame, and judgment toward one person does nothing but keep you trapped in the past. Until you let go of these uncomfortable emotions, they will continue to chip away at your daily mental health, decisions, and how you treat others. You can let these emotions go with a healthy dose of curiosity and compassion. "Maybe they" is a mindset cheat code that lets you engage these types of circuits in the brain and reframe the intentions behind actions to make them out to be less hurtful. Maybe they:

Were running late;

Didn't see me;

Were having a bad day;

Are having issues at home;

Didn't know;

Were hungry;

Haven't slept;

Are burnt out.

"Maybe they" forces you to question and edit the negative story playing in your head so you can replace it with a more curious and compassionate narrative, one where you assume the other person has positive intentions, and allows you to perceive their actions as less personal or hurtful. It allows you to consider that the person who hurt you might have just been unaware, scared, unsure, or simply struggling to do their best in this crazy game of life.

It doesn't mean you become a pushover and stop holding people accountable. It simply means allowing yourself to let go of the emotions that are clouding your perspective and preventing you from responding to how you're feeling in a meaningful way.

OCTOBER, Day 185: Trust Recession

Do you trust your peers and colleagues? If you answered no to this question, then you're not alone. According to a recent study of 5,400 workers, trust between employees fell the longer they were apart from each other during the pandemic. In May 2020, trust levels were fairly high; however, by October 2020, "the employees' degree of confidence in one another was down substantially." To make matters worse, 60% of managers doubted that remote workers performed better at home and employee-surveillance software has risen by more than 50%. Jerry Useem, who wrote about this study in *The Atlantic*, labeled this the "Trust Recession".[2]

It would be easy to assume "lack of connection" is driving this trust recession, but in reality it's more likely due to rising levels of stress and fear inside and outside the workplace. It's very hard to trust others when we don't feel safe. When fear dominates the workplace, we spend more time and energy fighting internal battles with each other than we do working together to outperform competitors.

The solution to solving mistrust within teams is not investing into more tools to measure how long someone is online or forcing people back to the office so they can collaborate. It's supporting better mental health and fostering psychological safety within teams remotely, two factors that lead to more compassion, empathy, transparency, and candor among team members, the prerequisites for trust. In an increasingly more uncertain and complex world, you need to be able to trust the people on your team if you want to be in a position to perform your best.

OCTOBER, Day 186: HALT

It can be hard to be empathetic or help others when we're feeling anxious. When this happens we need to remember to HALT. This is a popular acronym taught by therapists that helps us quickly answer a series of questions and identify the root cause of anxiety:

H - Are you hungry?

Hunger is one of our most primal needs. When we're hungry, our body goes into survival mode, making it hard to focus on anything else until this need is satisfied. Solution: find something to eat.

A - Are you angry?

Anger can often occur when we feel out of control, helpless, or leading with the wrong expectations. Solution: If you're upset about a situation, make a list of what you *can* control and what you *cannot* control about the situation. Then revisit the exercise on Day 95: Why Are You Angry?.

L - Are you lonely?

When we're lonely or feeling disconnected, empathy takes a back seat. Solution: Prioritize a detox from social media and replace the time spent scrolling actually talking with friends and family in person or over the phone.

T - Are you tired?

Sleep is the best natural medicine we have. One night of good night's rest has the power to help us regain perspective, feel more in control, and feel a little more safe. Solution: Prioritize good sleep hygiene and get to bed at a reasonable time this evening. Also a short nap can help too if you can fit it into your day.

If you've had a tough time emotionally connecting with buyers and colleagues today, remember to check your buckets to ensure your basic needs are being met first. Make it easy to remember to HALT throughout the day by putting it on a sticky note that is visible in your workspace.

OCTOBER, Day 187: Be Kind to Each Other

It can be hard to be kind to others while working remotely, so it got me thinking; when was the last time you did a good deed for a fellow salesperson on your team that goes beyond what you normally do on a daily basis? If it has been a while, it's time to get creative. It will not only help improve the mental health of your colleagues, but it will benefit you as well.

Studies show when you perform one random act of kindness a day, it reduces stress, anxiety, and depression in both you and your colleague.[3] Our acts of kindness release endorphins in the brain such as serotonin that helps you relax, lowers pain, and makes you feel good. Oxytocin is also released, which lowers blood pressure and builds a closer connection with the person you're helping.

Today, start brainstorming some random acts of kindness you can do for someone on your team. Here are some ideas to help you get started: Send them one of your favorite books. Offer to cover their workload for an hour so they can relax. Have lunch from their favorite spot delivered. Donate a meal to a local food bank on their behalf. Send them a handwritten note saying you appreciate them. What else can you add to the list? Try doing one a day for a week and see how you feel.

OCTOBER, Day 188: Did I Matter?

Why do sales organizations make it so damn hard to build a legacy at their company? It's literally one of the best and easiest things they can do to improve sales performance and culture.

We as humans want to matter. We want to know that grinding every single day in sales matters and that we were here. But it's hard to matter when every month your hard work is washed away and erased when the dashboard gets reset to zero. There is no opportunity to build a legacy that matters within the company. No opportunity to say, "Wow, I did that. I mattered to this company" and feel proud of your accomplishments when that day finally comes and you decide to leave the company. Instead, most salespeople leave companies and think: "Well, that was three and a half years of my life. Did I matter? Did I make a difference? Does the company even care that I was here?"

Feeling unimportant or devalued or worthless feels horrible. Salespeople show up and grind every single day, and their mental health is affected on a weekly basis while selling for a company. The least a sales organization can do is do a better job of recognizing them. To start, here are some ideas to show salespeople they mattered: Create a Hall of Fame to remember top salespeople of the past. Keep Lifetime Revenue and key accomplishments visible at all times. Assign team captains voted on by their peers. Finally, take the time to show a salesperson how much they mattered when they do decide to leave, by sharing a farewell package outlining the impact they made. These types of actions will do more for building a strong sales culture than any cake or open bar ever will.

OCTOBER, Day 189: Fix Yourself First

With all the clients, colleagues, partners, and family members you're trying to help right now, you might be suffering from "empathy burnout." When this happens it can become extremely hard to be compassionate and generous to others.

What's the solution to empathy burnout? Do something nice for *yourself.* If you're a highly empathetic person, it is very easy to get caught up in helping friends, family, colleagues, and strangers. You can quite literally *feel* their pain, and as a result you totally forget about the most important person in all of this, *you.*

With digital and social media bombarding us with a constant supply of bad news and issues that require our attention, it can be easy to feel like Atlas from Greek Mythology, trying to hold up a world that keeps getting heavier and heavier. Don't try to be Atlas. It's okay to step away and take care of yourself every now and then. This does not make you a bad person.

You have to remember that if you invest all of your energy into fixing other people, you'll have no energy left to fix yourself. Fix yourself *first,* and then get to work fixing the world. When you're the best version of yourself, you'll have the best chance to actually start helping others in a meaningful way. Do something extra nice for yourself today that will help you rest and recover. You deserve it.

OCTOBER, Day 190: Hope in Sales

Salespeople have the challenging task of balancing "false" hope of deals closing and using this extremely powerful human defense mechanism to protect mental health. Throughout my career I've had several managers and leaders tell me that I should not use hope in sales, that being hopeful will lead to me chasing dead deals, but they're wrong.

Hope is extremely important in fostering resiliency and mental stability when facing negative experiences such as buyers ghosting, deals falling through, and missing targets. Being hopeful means that you believe that there are multiple ways for you to succeed or close a deal within sales. When one pathway into an account becomes blocked, you can be flexible and find a new way. It means you're more likely to perceive failure as a learning opportunity and the result of a poor strategy, rather than a character flaw you cannot bounce back from. In a recent study that measured personality strengths over the course of the year, hope emerged as the only resilience factor that protected well-being during highly emotional events.[4]

Next time you encounter a setback in sales, remember to use hope. Accept the setback. Learn from it. Then find a new path forward. To avoid the valley of "false" hope that many salespeople find themselves in, remember that hope without action, is *not* hope. If you're hoping a deal will close, brainstorm one action you can take to increase the chances of it closing. These actions might involve sending a buyer a helpful piece of information, removing friction in the purchasing process, or offering to join your buyer in an internal meeting with their manager. Anything that removes uncertainty or discomfort, which may be making the buyer anxious.

OCTOBER Endnotes

1. "Sleep Improves Sales Productivity & Revenue: A Case Study." Rise Science. https://www.risescience.com/blog/sleep-sales-productivity-revenue.
2. Useem, J. "The End of Trust." *The Atlantic.* November 24, 2021. https://www.theatlantic.com/magazine/archive/2021/12/trust-recession-economy/620522/.
3. Sweet, J. "How Random Acts of Kindness Can Boot Your Health During The Pandemic." *verywellmind.* February 10, 2021. https://www.verywellmind.com/how-random-acts-of-kindness-can-boost-your-health-5105301.
4. Goodman, F., Disabato, D., Kashdan, T, and Machell, K. "Personality Strengths as Resilience: A One-Year Multiwave Study." *Journal of Personality* 85(3). February 2016. https://www.researchgate.net/publication/295259707_Personality_Strengths_as_Resilience_A_One-Year_Multiwave_Study.

NOVEMBER

NOVEMBER, Day 191: Buyer Mental Health

Have you ever considered the mental health of your buyer or customer? If not, this needs to be top of mind during your next demo or client meeting.

Every successful salesperson knows that asking really good questions is the key to uncovering pain points and blind spots the buyer may not be fully aware of. Then we as salespeople take that pain point and show them how much money they're losing, how much time they're wasting, how poor the quality of their results are, how little control they actually have, how unsafe they actually are, how much risk they actually face, and how big of an unknown threat they're facing. We turn their world upside down. The best sellers do this because they genuinely want to improve the lives of the people they sell to and not manipulate them into buying a product they don't need to make a quick buck.

However, we have to remember that this process is likely going to make the buyer *anxious* and *uncomfortable*. If you're going to intentionally scare someone like this, then you better have a solution and process that is also going to help calm them down, a *really* good story that helps the buyer see themselves as a hero who will make a difference by facing these fears.

It's this last piece I see most manipulative sellers miss. They simply don't consider the buyer's feelings throughout their process and leave them making decisions based on fear. Instead, think about how you can make the buyer feel curious and empowered throughout your sales process because that's when they'll be motivated to change.

NOVEMBER, Day 192: Mastery Manipulation

We have to be careful which external workplace cultures are influencing our own. For example, Wall Street takes the cake for one of the most deceptive things I've heard recently. When a brokerage executive was asked how they train new hires, they responded with:

> "Well, if you think about the rule that it takes about 10,000 hours to master something. And if you think about someone who takes a more traditional route working 8 hours per day, it's going to take you about 5 years to have a base level mastery. On Wall Street, it's more like 12 hours a day, 6 days a week, which cuts you down to about 2.5 years before you become mastered in something."

This is extremely manipulative to say to a fresh graduate who doesn't know any better. Executives like this are trying to disguise this toxic culture and harsh burnout practice of 72-plus-hour weeks behind the label of "mastery." Even worse, I have since seen this statement posted across several other news outlets, claiming this as a best practice and reinforcing it as a norm new graduates should expect going forward, norms that easily get adopted by sales teams outside of the financial services sector.

As a community of mental health advocates, we need to be aware of how damaging a PR campaign like this can be to future generations and our own teams. If executives preaching this type of nonsense had ever picked up a book on sleep, stress management, mental health, how the brain learns, or peak performance, they would realize that working 72-plus-hour weeks without proper recovery time is about the worst possible strategy to master anything. My guess is they have read these books though—they just don't care.

Every sales organization in the world is blessed with a batch of fresh graduates they have the opportunity to hire from each semester. It doesn't mean it's ethical nor efficient to burn and churn whomever doesn't make the cut. If you have a batch of new sales hires starting soon, it's our responsibility to teach them how to have long, successful careers within sales and avoid burnout in the short term.

NOVEMBER, Day 193: Super Mario

Sales teams can learn a lot about motivation and how to design engaging sales cultures from Super Mario 64. Structurally the game changed a lot about the gaming industry, which helped make playing video games more fun going forward.

Prior to Super Mario 64, the majority of video games were roughly structured in the following way: Players start with a set of "lives." Playing earns the player points. Doing good things earns lives/points, and doing bad things loses lives/points. Losing all your lives means game over. Leaderboards publicly display your points, and losing the game restarts you at zero.

Within this structure and game design, rarely was the purpose for playing the game to "beat it." It was to beat your friends by scoring more points than them.

The way old video games were structured for players is very similar to how current sales environments are structured for sellers. Most salespeople are only as good as their last "game," or month. At the end of each month/ quarter they face the crushing sensation of restarting back at zero. There is also constant pressure to earn more "lives" and "points" in the form of closing deals. This allows salespeople to keep their job so they can keep selling (playing the game) and avoid the humiliation that comes with being at the bottom of the dashboard. When you run out of lives in sales, it's game over, which means you're likely going to be looking for a new job.

Due to the way this game is set up, fear of failure is rampant, which means salespeople are always looking for shortcuts, rarely share leads, and almost never collaborate on deals. Those of us working in sales have a lot to learn from the game designers of Super Mario 64. The changes they made changed gaming forever, by essentially removing "lives" from the game. They still had them, and if you did too many bad things, Mario would die, but the most important change game designers made was you didn't have to start back at zero or at the beginning of the game when you died. You restarted close to where you failed so you could try again.

This allowed players to take more risks, explore levels more freely, and find creative solutions to problems they would not have found otherwise. It also resulted in friends working together to share turns, secrets, and best practices. Game designers also removed the heavy use of leaderboards and instead made in-game achievements more clear, purposeful, rewarded character development, and made each level feel new and unique, which created a more meaningful experience for the player overall. This meant players focused all of their attention on the task at hand—playing and "beating the game," rather than worrying about "beating their friends" and avoiding humiliation outside of the game. As a result Super Mario 64 (and future video games) became intrinsically motivating to play, which boosted engagement, time spent playing, and overall performance by players.

The design lessons the sales industry can adopt from the gaming industry are this: (1) Make it safe for reps to fail. (2) Stop using fear and "lives." (3) Stop starting at zero each month. (4) Keep lifetime revenue sold visible. (5) Dial back the dashboards. (6) Make career progress clear. (7) Reward personal development. (8) Make sales targets *meaningful*. (9) Lower team competition. (10) Encourage collaboration and sharing. Which of these changes do you think would benefit your sales organization the most?

NOVEMBER, Day 194: Failure in Sales

Successful sales careers are built on failure. Thousands and thousands of micro-failures such as: embarrassing yourself in front of your peers on a bad call, asking the wrong questions, forgetting your pitch, calling the wrong person, accidentally hitting send on an email that is not ready, pushing too hard, not pushing enough, quoting the wrong price in a proposal, name-dropping an irrelevant client, following up at the wrong time, calling the prospect by the wrong name, mishandling an objection, being too afraid to call the decision maker, double-booking your demos, not prospecting enough and letting your pipeline go stale, forecasting incorrectly, losing a deal you should have won, or being underprepared for a meeting.

Today, be grateful for all of your mistakes or failures, and practice some self-compassion. Compassion for yourself means you don't need to be delusional about your progress or feel incompetent when you're making mistakes and trying to learn. Gratitude during these moments will help protect your mental health and keep you on the path to success. This will help you stay present and focused on your next call and leave negative experiences in the past.

Keep falling, and keep getting back up. You're learning and getting better.

Much like labeling our emotions can help us feel calmer, labeling our failure can help us show more compassion to ourselves. Scan here and use a failure spectrum to do this effectively.

NOVEMBER, Day 195: "Feeling Lucky"

You know that feeling you get when you find a lucky penny on the ground? I still catch myself saying, "Must be my lucky day" when it happens. What's fascinating is that positive things then randomly start happening. Someone holds a door open for me. That prospect I've been chasing responds to my email. And I catch the streetcar that I thought I'd miss. I think, "Such a good day! I'm so lucky, right?"

Wrong. Luck doesn't exist, but "feeling lucky" does.

The random act of finding a penny primed my brain to start "feeling lucky," which made me more optimistic and perceptive of positive experiences happening all around me. Someone holding the door, the prospect responding to my email, and catching the streetcar all would have happened anyway, but because I was "feeling lucky" I actually noticed them. Because I noticed them, my happiness benefited.

"Lucky" things and positive experiences are happening to salespeople every day. We're just really bad at noticing them when we're stuck thinking about a bad call, stuck in morning traffic, or rehearsing a difficult performance review with our manager. Change this by finding your lucky penny to start an upward spiral. The first good thing you notice today—pause and acknowledge it. Tell yourself it's your lucky day, and then be mindful of how many other good things you start to notice.

NOVEMBER, Day 196: The Drivers

In January 2010, you could have bought one share of Salesforce for ~$15. In August 2021, the same share cost roughly $268.

The last decade has been dominated by an arms race in sales technology. Companies invested millions into new sales technologies in hopes of achieving greater productivity and increased sales performance, and it worked. Companies that could afford the best CRM, prospecting, market research, forecasting, calling, call recording, email automation, customer engagement, and sales intelligence software could build the perfect tech stack. They could build a sales engine that operated like a fast Ferrari, and with a Ferrari it didn't really matter what salesperson was driving it. With basic sales competency training, organizations could plug in and play drivers and still meet their growth targets. If the driver was sick, anxious, depressed, or burnt out, it was easy to simply replace them.

However, things have now changed, and it has become cheaper and easier to build a Ferrari than ever before. Targets continue to grow, and new sales enablement tools can no longer make up the difference. As a result, the next several decades in sales will be dominated by the drivers. Drivers who can drive their Ferraris the fastest, while making the fewest mistakes. Companies that take care of them will win. This means if you're a sales leader with a well-oiled machine, before investing into another flashy new sales technology, you're better off investing into a program that supports the mental health of your salespeople instead.

NOVEMBER, Day 197: Seeds of Growth

Every challenging experience you face is a seed that can help you grow. A missed sales target, rejected job interview, failed relationship, or a traumatizing health experience, these are all seeds and opportunities for growth.

But like a seed, these experiences require a gentle hand, dedication, effort, time, compassion, and nurturing in order to flourish. This is hard work, and it's much easier to bury, forget, and neglect these seeds. To pretend like they never happened or avoid these anxious experiences, and get back to neutral, as when things were comfortable, easy, and life was more manageable—back to the previous status quo. But it only takes one, two, or maybe three; a few seeds that grow and fundamentally change who you are. When you do what's hard, put in the work, and embrace the emotional discomfort within these challenging experiences which help you learn, grow, and move forward.

This is when you start to see it. You see your anxiety not as your enemy but as your friend. It's there to tell you when you have found a seed and when you're outside your comfort zone. Before, you were afraid of these feelings, but now you know better. You start to work with your new friend, rather than against it. You use it to seek out discomfort, to grow, and to be happy.

NOVEMBER, Day 198: Planning to Miss

Three statistics that you should be thinking about today as you work toward your sales target:

1. **Power of a Plan**

    Robert Epstein, an American psychologist, surveyed 30,000 people in 30 countries and found that the most effective method for reducing stress is having a plan. Having a plan makes us feel in control because it forces us to think about how to overcome future obstacles.[1]

2. **More Than Half Miss Quota**

    In 2018, a report by Salesforce said 57% of sales reps were expected to miss their quotas. I wasn't able to find a more recent data point, but it's safe to assume this percentage has remained the same or increased given the rapid decline in mental health of salespeople.[2]

3. **Missing Quota Affects Mental Health**

    In a survey I conducted through Sales Health Alliance, 41% of sales-people listed "missing quota" as having one of the greatest impacts on their mental health, ahead of other stressors such as cold-calling, losing a deal, and restarting back at zero each month.

With these data points in mind, do you have a plan for when you miss your quota, which you can use to protect your mental health? It might not happen this month, this quarter, or this year, but odds are that it's going to happen at some point during your career. Making a plan now of what you'll do when you miss a target in the future will put you in control of the stressful event when it occurs. This will help prevent your emotional brain and bad habits from taking over in the moment. Create a step-by-step list of actions that you can follow to offload stress (i.e. go for a massage), reset your mind (i.e. journal about what happened), learn from the experience (i.e. pull out areas for improvement), and ask for help (i.e. talk to your manager about where you need more training or support).

NOVEMBER, Day 199: Story Editing

If you're new to sales, it's very easy to think, "I can't do this" or "I'm not right for sales" after a couple of bad calls or lost deals. Practicing self-compassion is a crucial part of achieving consistent success within sales. You can do this by changing the story playing in your head to something like, "It's okay to struggle right now—I'm just learning the ropes."

A study by Timothy Wilson at the University of Virginia showed that students who were able to reinterpret academic challenges and move thinking away from negative or self-defeating thoughts achieved better grades and were less likely to drop out.[3] He calls this process story editing. As a highly competitive salesperson, story editing can be extremely hard to do because you want to win—and win right away. Sales and learning a product takes time, which means there are significant advantages to going easy on yourself. Acknowledge there is a learning curve, and practicing self-compassion will help you ramp up much faster.

If you take a moment to close your eyes, pause, and listen to the voice in your head right now, what's it telling you today? Are the thoughts more positive or negative? Write them out on a piece of paper. For the thoughts that are more negative, you can edit your story by reframing them in a more positive light using phrases such as "I'm learning," "I'm trying my best," "I'm exactly where I need to be in the process," "I get stronger by doing hard things," or "It's just not my day, and I'll be better tomorrow."

NOVEMBER, Day 200: Instant Gratification

One of the biggest challenges sales leaders face today is battling the increasing number of new sales reps who have been primed for instant gratification. Society is teaching everyone that our desires can and should be fulfilled instantly: We can watch TV shows and movies instantly on Netflix. We can order something on Amazon and have it delivered the next day. We can match with strangers and set up dates within minutes. We can share information on social media and receive instant engagement. Many aspects of life that previously required skill, effort, and patience no longer do.

Sales doesn't work like this, and it is a very slow burn. It takes time, discipline, and practice to master and develop it into a skill. This process has become less common and forgotten in our daily lives. As a result, managing expectations of junior sales reps is one of the most important duties of any sales leader. Successfully doing so will help them keep things in perspective, encourage compassionate self-talk, and stabilize mental health during the bumpy sales road ahead.

One of the best ways leaders can do this is by scheduling regular meetings to reinforce that "success" for new reps is not measured by how many sales they close. Success is being measured on how quickly they're learning to do the right things in their control such as asking engaging questions to buyers, prospecting every day, and practicing their pitch. Encouraging a new rep build good habits such as these early, helps them fall in love with the feeling of making progress each day, rather than the gratification of closing a deal.

NOVEMBER, Day 201: Don't Speak Up

If you were to refilm the popular Netflix movie *Don't Look Up* to capture the mental health crisis instead of the climate crisis, it would be titled *Don't Speak Up.*

In the "2021 Mental Health in Sales Report" that we completed with UNCrushed and The Harris Consulting Group (mentioned earlier), we found only 41% of salespeople felt like they could be open and vulnerable with how they were feeling at work.

This is not enough.

Anyone who has worked in sales knows it can feel like an emotional roller coaster most days. If those emotions don't have a healthy outlet to be expressed, shared, and learned from, then boundaries, sleep, smart eating choices, exercise, fulfillment, happiness, relationships, mental health, and sales performance are all eroded over time.

Salespeople (and all employees) need workplace environments that allow them to be vulnerable. It's how optimal mental performance is achieved. Leaders set the vulnerability tone within their teams, and those who lead with vulnerability create safer spaces for reps to use their voice and express what they're feeling. If you're feeling overwhelmed today or have made a mistake recently, use it as an opportunity to be more vulnerable with your team. The longer we don't look up and don't speak up, the closer that asteroid gets to destroying the culture and profits we've worked so hard to build.

Don't wait until it's too late.

NOVEMBER, Day 202: Rehearsal Loop

Ever wonder why your mind won't stop racing at the end of a busy day? Neuroscientist Daniel Levitin says[4]: "When you're worried about something and your gray matter is afraid you may forget, it engages a cluster of brain regions referred to as the rehearsal loop; and you keep worrying and worrying."

To stop this, Levitin says you should write your thoughts down and make a plan for tomorrow. Rather than worrying about forgetting what time your big pitch is tomorrow, what you'll say, or what you have to bring to the meeting, write it all down before you shut down from work the day before. Write down the time of your meeting, write down a checklist of what you need to bring or have prepared, and write down what you'll say on practice cue cards to review in the morning. Doing this will allow your brain to focus on what is important: relaxing with friends and family at home and getting a good night's rest.

Try this with a big meeting or demo you have coming this week. Make sure you do all the prep work the afternoon before, rather than rushing the morning of the meeting. Did you sleep better? Were you less anxious beforehand? How did you perform? If you slept, entered the meeting calmly, and performed well, then you successfully prevented a rehearsal loop.

NOVEMBER, Day 203: Small Actions Matter Most

Optimizing your mental health rarely happens with one large sweeping action. It happens from a collection of tiny actions you choose to take or not take each day that stack on top of each to make you feel better or worse.

The personalized monthly report I get from WHOOP has made this clear. For those unfamiliar with WHOOP, it's a well-being tracker that you wear on your wrist, which captures various health metrics (think of a Fitbit on steroids). It also includes a daily journal you fill out each morning. The journal asks you questions about your daily behaviors and then uses the health data it collects to calculate the estimated impact those behaviors have on your recovery score. This recovery score quantifies your body's readiness to perform inside and outside the workplace and ranges from 0 to 99%. Below are some of the metrics and insights I've learned about myself:

Actions positively affecting my recovery score:

Proper sleep = +6%

Stretching = +5%

Breathwork = +4%

Intermittent fasting = +4%

Total = +19%

Actions negatively affecting my recovery score:

High-strain day = −8%

Late meal = −5%

Alcohol = −4%

Low hydration = −3%

Total = −20%

As you can see, the impact of each action is *very* small overall, but when added together, there could be a massive swing of +/− 39% on my body's readiness to perform, depending on the actions I take or don't take each day. Having access to this kind of data has helped me learn two key things I take into my day each morning:

1. **Focus on the small wins:** If you're struggling or experiencing burnout, start thinking about making small changes to your daily routine first, rather than one big change such as quitting your job or breaking up with someone.

2. **Discipline and consistency is the key:** When building a new habit, it's okay to miss or cheat one day, but make a rule with yourself that you're never allowed to miss twice in a row. This will help you balance compassion and accountability when trying something new.

NOVEMBER, Day 204: Buyer Ghosting

Buyers have been known to ghost salespeople from time to time. It happens when a buyer simply stops responding and disappears during the sales process. Typically it happens something like this: The rep and the buyer are connecting, interest is established, and emails and calls are traded back and forth. Things are going great, and sometimes there is even a proposal on the table, and the buyer has said, "Yes, this all looks good to me—let's connect in a few days and move forward."

Then *poof*—the buyer vanishes like a ghost. They stop responding to emails, taking calls, and seemingly fall off the face of the earth. Worst part is they disappear and give the sales rep no indication of what happened or what went wrong, which creates a high degree of uncertainty. Uncertainty that fuels anxiety and self-doubt in the future.

In one survey, I found that 27% of salespeople who have inbound and outbound responsibilities listed buyer ghosting as one of the top three stressors that negatively affects their mental health. To learn why this affects our mental health and how we can prevent buyer ghosting from becoming a common occurrence, I've created a helpful article to walk you through the steps.

Ghosts become less scary when you learn how to become a ghostbuster, so scan here to get started.

NOVEMBER, Day 205: Challenging Experiences

I'm super grateful for these three challenging experiences I faced on my path to starting Sales Health Alliance.

1. Getting Laid Off

Back in March 2018, Facebook drastically changed the amount of data their API provided to third parties overnight in response to the Cambridge Analytica scandal. This resulted in layoffs (including myself) at the social media analytics company I was working at and forced me outside my comfort zone.

2. Getting Testicular Cancer

Before being diagnosed with testicular cancer in July of 2018, I was committed to looking for a new job and on the fence about being an entrepreneur. This diagnosis gave me clarity, perspective, and urgency to jump into the deep end. Life is short, and the timing will never be perfect, so I may as well try and live with no regrets.

3. Living with (at Times, Debilitating) Anxiety

Early on in my sales career I was embarrassed by my anxiety and panic attacks, but over time I've grown to realize how important they have been in my life. They have given me meaning and a challenge I'm passionate about solving. Something I can relate to and connect over with almost everyone. I'm grateful to have met so many other salespeople and mental health advocates who are starting to change sales cultures for the better. The biggest thing I've learned since becoming an entrepreneur is you can find the good in every experience you face. Challenging experiences in particular offer the best opportunities for growth. You just have to be compassionate to yourself and remember to look for it. What challenging experiences have you had in your life that you can be grateful for?

NOVEMBER, Day 206: The PIP

Nine months into my first sales role I was placed on a performance improvement plan (PIP). After my first four months of exceeding my target, I began to struggle with my mental health. I had no idea how to manage the daily ups and downs of the sales grind. I had also just moved into my first apartment, and after five months of missing target and commission checks I was anxious about paying bills. To cope with the anxiety, I was drinking and partying, but I didn't know that was only making things worse, because everyone around me was doing it too. I couldn't sleep and had panic attacks that resulted in hospital visits in the middle of the night. I also didn't share any of this with my employer out of fear, because I couldn't even describe what I was feeling to the people closest to me.

Then came the PIP and an unrealistic target no one in the company had ever hit. I was engulfed in anger, but I used that anger to outwork everyone around me and exceeded my target. I then exploded past my next three sales targets. I set records and became the top salesperson in the North American office; to "reward" me, the company flew me to the head office in London.

But then I left. In the midst of an extremely difficult time in my life, not a single manager stopped to ask, "Are you okay?" and preferred to use fear as a motivational tool. This proved they didn't care about my career or well-being long term, and I wanted to work for people who cared.

The moral of the story? If a sales rep has shown success and is now struggling, show them you care and ask whether they are okay. They'll rarely forgive and never forget the person who gave them a PIP. Is this how you'd want to be remembered as a sales leader?

NOVEMBER, Day 207: Becoming a Chameleon

One of the most insightful messages I've received came from a rep named Andrew who said, "If I can be a chameleon with my customers, management can be a chameleon with their salesforce." I think this one sentence succinctly sums up a major area for improvement in sales leadership today.

Top individual performers who get promoted to management usually default into "this is how you sell" mode and proceed to impose their personal style on to their teams. When it doesn't work, new managers tend to become obsessed with metrics. I have certainly been guilty of this in the past, and it often leads to frustration, micromanagement, and declining mental health for the entire team.

When new managers get promoted, they need to keep selling. Now, they're no longer selling to customers, they're selling to their reps and using their sales skills to build trust, tell stories, ask good questions, provide value, and help them overcome challenges they're facing. But more importantly, identifying what each rep on their team is motivated by. Their *why*.

Like most customers, individual reps are smart but won't necessarily know what motivates them when times get tough. Is it money? Family or a loved one? Or perhaps deeply caring about the product they sell? As a new manager, it's your job to learn, adapt, and sell, to be a chameleon. In doing so, you will also be building the foundation for supportive mental health conversations.

NOVEMBER, Day 208: The First Call

Making that first call as a new rep at a new company on the sales floor is one of the most terrifying moments for any sales rep. Not only do you have to call a total stranger to talk to them about a product you hardly know yet, but you also have an audience of well-trained colleagues sitting around you. They pretend that they're not listening or paying attention, but they usually are. They're curious and want to know how talented you are. They want to know if you are someone they'll be competing against for promotions and sales accolades.

When you're in a situation like this, your body senses that the risk of making a mistake and embarrassing yourself is *high*, a nightmare for anxiety and mental health. Your breathing will quicken, your mouth might dry up, your voice may tremble a little bit, and your hands will start to sweat, none of which is ideal for making that first call.

So what do you do? Here are three strategies that really helped me that you can use to calm your nerves:

1) If you don't use a script, at least have some talking points, questions, and the main objection handles you intend to face ready. Practice reading over it. This is your plan, and we've already learned how they help to reduce stress.
2) Try lowering your stress response by inhaling for four seconds and exhaling for six seconds. Repeat for six to ten breaths. Making your exhales longer than your inhales is a proven way to slow down your heart rate.
3) Whoever answers the phone, use your situation to your advantage to build rapport: "I'm really excited you answered—I just started at my company, so I'm a little nervous, but you're the first person I get to speak with. How are you today?"

If it's the first day for someone on your team today, be mindful of when they start making their first calls. Keep them motivated with some positive feedback because it will mean the world to them in a new environment.

NOVEMBER, Day 209: Jeff Goldblum

When I was watching the Jeff Goldblum docuseries on Disney+, it was hard to not be utterly mesmerized by his level of positivity. His emotions and energy were so infectious to everyone around him that people (even total strangers) couldn't help but like him. So how does he do it?

1. Obsessive Curiosity

He is obsessively curious and wants to learn about anything and everything around him, so he keeps asking questions. Why did you do X? What do you think about Y? Tell me about Z. His curiosity is never satisfied with the answer he receives to his first question, so he keeps asking. This forces people to keep talking about their interests, which builds trust and friendships *fast*.

2. He Shows He Cares

By asking questions and being genuinely engaged in conversation, he shows the person he is speaking with that he cares and he's listening. As a result, he can't help but be totally present in every conversation. He gives people 100% of his attention, which rarely happens these days, especially if you're a movie star with a big ego.

Today, I encourage you to try being a little more like Jeff Goldblum in your interactions with clients, colleagues, and family. Become obsessively curious about their lives. This will force you to be present and take attention off the self-conscious thoughts and self-doubt that usually hold you back from engaging in a meaningful way.

NOVEMBER, Day 210: The Off-Season

If you're a sales leader planning to say something such as "If you have a slow December, you'll have a slow January," don't do it—it's tone-deaf. Almost every salesperson is going into December hoping for a "quieter" month, and this feeling is likely a sign that they're experiencing burnout and need time to rest and recover.

Every professional athlete in the world has an off-season, time when they can rest, get their mind right, and recover from the stress their body was under during competition, which allows them to come back the following season faster, stronger, and more resilient.

Salespeople are corporate athletes, and they also need an off-season. No, I'm not saying this is a time to stop working, drink, do drugs, eat unhealthy, and binge-watch Netflix all month. It's a time for salespeople to get their body and mind ready for next season.

- Catch up on self-care;
- Make a plan for January;
- Prioritize self-development;
- Get your CRM and pipeline in order;
- Do something nice for your customers.

If every salesperson on your team read a different personal development book in December, then applied it to their sales process, and trained others on the team, what would that wealth of knowledge do to your team? Would all these new ideas give the team hope? Start thinking long term.

NOVEMBER Endnotes

1. Pelaez, M. "Play Your Way to Less Stress, More Happiness." *Time Magazine.* May 31, 2011. https://healthland.time.com/2011/05/31/study-25-of-happiness-depends-on-stress-management/.
2. Bova, T. "26 Sales Statistics That Prove Selling Is Changing." Salesforce. January 25, 2019. https://www.salesforce.com/blog/15-sales-statistics/.
3. Cook, G. "How to Improve Your Life with 'Story Editing.'" *Scientific American.* September 13, 2011. https://www.scientificamerican.com/article/how-to-improve-your-life-with-story-editing/.
4. Levitin, D. (2015). *The Organized Mind: Thinking straight in the age of information overload.* Viking.

DECEMBER

DECEMBER, Day 211: Your Inner Citadel

There is a common misconception that resilience is built during hard times, but it's not. It's built during the good times. It's why people who are healthy and take good care of their body recover from surgery faster. It's why athletes who train their physical health during the off-season get injured less during the season. It's why salespeople who prioritize their mental health outside of working hours bounce back from rejection and setbacks faster. And it's why people who had invested time into learning mindset, stress-management, and mental health best practices before the COVID-19 pandemic managed better through lockdown.

The Stoics call this process "building your Inner Citadel," which is your inner fortress that no adversity can break. As Ryan Holiday explains in *The Daily Stoic*, "During the good times, we strengthen ourselves and our bodies so that during the difficult times, we can depend on it. We reinforce our inner fortress so we can depend on it later."[1]

January 1 will likely bring some difficult times:

- New year;
- New quota;
- New responsibilities;
- New expectations.

Don't wait and enter these stressful times mentally out of shape. The preparation starts now so be intentional with strengthening your Inner Citadel this month.

DECEMBER, Day 212: Building Empathy

To be successful in sales and life you need to be empathetic. The most empathetic people are sensitive and care a lot about their customers, colleagues, and company. The easiest way to burn out empaths (highly empathetic people) is to not be sensitive to their feelings and neglect the effort they invest on a daily basis. This tends to happen more frequently if they are treated like a number that leaders feel like they can always give more to because empaths often don't push back.

If you're a sales leader, consider how you're protecting empaths by spending time building healthy empathy into your sales team culture by considering these questions: How are you teaching empathy to the salespeople on your team? How can you help your team become more empathetic to one another? How can you be a more empathetic leader? Some exercises to have in your toolkit and that will help build more team empathy are as follows:

1. **Switch shoes:** During the next team debate or argument, try having the people involved switch shoes and debate on behalf of the side they're opposed to. Healthy empathy requires learning how to consider multiple points of view, and there is no better time to work on this skill than when we strongly agree or disagree with something.

2. **Revisit your buyer's journey:** Everyone on your team can stretch their empathy muscles by walking through the current buyer's journey as a team. If you were in a buyer's shoes and were to land on your website or read the copy in a cold email, what would you think, feel, and action in response? What experience would you have? Is this the experience you want your buyers and prospects to have?

3. **Team gratitude:** Build a team gratitude practice in which team members regularly share one person they're grateful for on their team and how that person made them feel. For example, "I'm grateful for Jimmy today who helped me practice my pitch for five minutes. He helped me *feel* more confident going into my calls today."

4. **Cross-functional appreciation:** If your sales team works closely with a cross-functional team such as customer success or partnerships team, do something kind for someone you appreciate in a different department. As we've learned, acts of kindness go a long way in improving our own mental health as well as the person we're helping.

DECEMBER, Day 213: Law of the Lever

Do you know how to resolve conflicts you face in sales? Whether it's inner conflict with our thoughts, feelings, and emotions that are spiraling out of control when we're anxious or an external conflict such as a disagreement with a partner, friend, or buyer, there's no question that trying to resolve conflict can be extremely challenging and have a dramatic impact on our daily mental health. As a result, many of us avoid conflict at all cost.

But conflict doesn't need to be hard, scary, or burdensome. Sometimes all you need to do is shift your mindset, and an easy way to remember to do this is to learn about "the law of the lever." The law of the lever is a principle created by Greek mathematician, physicist, engineer, inventor, and astronomer Archimedes. He is famous for saying, "Give me a place to stand on, and I will move the Earth." Archimedes used this principle to demonstrate how we can use a lever to amplify our force and lift objects far heavier than we could have otherwise. Depending on the positioning of our fulcrum, we can make a heavy stone easier or harder to lift.

We can use this law metaphorically to explain why navigating conflict is so difficult when we experience challenging emotions such as anger, fear, and shame. These emotions shift us into a defensive mindset in which we're motivated to avoid conflict, shifting our "fulcrum" away from conflict. Similar to trying to lift a heavy rock with no leverage, resolving conflict in a defensive mindset becomes stressful and usually hopeless.

The good news is we're always in control of our mindset, just like we're in control of where we place our fulcrum. We can use emotions such as compassion, curiosity, love, and empathy to create a pro-social mindset that motivates us to approach conflict. In doing so, we move our fulcrum closer to conflict, which creates leverage and makes it less stressful to resolve.

If resolving conflict means we need to become more curious, compassionate, empathetic, and loving, then the big question we have is how do we create these emotions? Answer: We ask good questions.

Much like how we ask good questions to defensive buyers to make them more curious about what we're selling, we can ask ourselves good questions when we're feeling defensive that help us become more curious in resolving conflict. Here are some questions to help you get started: Why might they be feeling angry, anxious, afraid, or ashamed? How did I contribute to making them feel this way? What other factors could be making them feel this way? What do I love most about this person? How have they helped me in the past? How can I go easier on them? What's one nice thing I can do for them?

So next time you're experiencing any conflict, pause and ask yourself: Are you using your mindset to create leverage? If not, then use the questions above as prompts to interrupt your defensive mindset and journal for 10 minutes. This exercise should help you leverage your thinking and approach conflict with a pro-social mindset that is fueled by curiosity, compassion, empathy, and love.

 Need a good visual to help you remember the law of the lever? Scan here to see how changing your mindset changes the position of your lever to create more leverage.

DECEMBER, Day 214: Bad Is Stronger than Good

"Bad is stronger than good" is a phenomenon researchers have been studying for years. It refers to the data that proves the psychological effects of bad things outweigh the effect of good things on humans.[2] For example, research on relationships shows that the presence or absence of negative behaviors is more strongly related to the quality (bad or good) of the relationship, than the presence or absence of positive behaviors. This means increasing positive behaviors will have less of an impact on the quality of the relationship compared to decreasing the frequency of negative behaviors.

We can put this research to good use in sales by applying it to several different areas. For example, by putting more focus on reducing negative client experiences (i.e. removing product bugs), we increase the chances of closing a sale more than increasing positive client experiences in our sales process (i.e. running a better demo). Within a team, reducing negative behaviors causing burnout (bullying, unachievable targets, working late, etc.) will do more for improving your team's mental health than a positive behavior such as investing into a wellness initiative. Finally, this also applies to individuals and for example, if you're a daily smoker who is trying to become healthier, reducing the frequency of cigarettes you smoke will do more for improving your health than something positive such as eating healthy.

Today, focus on bringing more awareness to your bad habits, toxic relationships, and negative things in your life that are holding you back. Rather than investing more time into good things, good habits, and good friends, focus on removing the bad ones first. That's a more efficient way to move forward.

DECEMBER, Day 215: Keeping It Objective

When we're struggling with anxiety, it can be hard to talk about it in the workplace because we don't want to damage our career. Feeling anxious also makes it incredibly difficult to deliver a clear message that doesn't involve blaming others.

Not making it personal and offering solutions is the key to helping people better understand your stressors, which means we want to avoid saying things such as: "My boss stresses me out," "I can't work with her, and I want to quit," "He is a horrible person, and I can't sleep at night." These are personal statements that will make most people defensive because they're unclear. When describing how you're feeling, you need to make it *objective*, instead of *subjective*, and you can do this by referencing specific behaviors:

"When you (*X behavior*), it makes me feel (*your emotion*), which means/because I (*consequence/impact*). Can we (*possible solution + benefit*) instead?"

Example #1: "When you send me an email on Sunday night, I start to feel anxious about the week ahead, which means I sleep poorly and get off to a slow start. Can we save weekend emails for Monday morning so I'm more productive at the start of the week?"

Example #2: "When you ask me about my pipeline at the end of the day, my mind starts to race after work because I don't have time to act on your feedback until the next day. Can we schedule pipeline discussions around lunch time so I can act on your coaching in the afternoon?"

Taking time to label an unpleasant emotion you're feeling and connecting it to a behavior someone else has taken will force you to slow down and respond logically, rather than react emotionally.

DECEMBER, Day 216: Finding the Present

Salespeople will rarely do something unless they know why taking a certain action is important to them. For example, when a non-salesperson says, "You should try meditating," and the reason why is something vague, overly spiritual, or unclear, salespeople will be unlikely to try it. I typically encourage salespeople to get into mediation by saying the following things:

From the moment you're born, to the moment you die, your breath is with you. For the better part of most days, salespeople are thinking about the future or thinking about the past. When you're worried about future sales targets, your breath changes. When you're worried about deals lost in the past, your breath changes. Happiness is found in the present, and you've experienced this happiness when you've felt chills at a concert, when your mind has lit up while kissing your significant other, or the euphoria you've felt after closing a deal. During these moments, your anxious mind has switched off, and every sense in your body is focused on keeping you present. Changes to your breath is an early warning system you need to be more aware of if you want to perform your best in sales. Meditation teaches you how to become mindful of changes in your breath during stressful situations and teaches you how to connect with something that has been part of you for your entire life—your breath.

Meditation is a powerful grounding exercise that, when practiced, will pull you out of the past or future and into the now, an action you can take at any time to calm your anxiety, which will make future targets less scary and make past failures hurt less. You can regain perspective and rediscover your happiness so you can be grateful for what you have in the moment.

DECEMBER, Day 217: How Supported Do You Feel?

There is one very simple thing all sales leaders can do each week to build a more supportive mental health environment that will improve team performance. It starts with asking how supported sales reps feel each week, and here is an easy way to do this effectively:

1. Create a Google form;
2. Make it optional to share their name;
3. Ask these two questions:
   a. How supported did you feel from a mental health standpoint this week? (Scale 1–5)
   b. What's one action I could have taken as your manager to improve this score?
4. Repeat every single week.

It's literally that simple, and following these steps as a leader will provide you with consistent feedback to help you learn what your team needs from you as a leader to be more supportive. Think about it, we *all* have blind spots as humans, and you ask your sales team about their metrics and revenue *every* single day. The very least you can do is ask whether they feel supported at least once a week so you can continually learn and improve as a leader.

DECEMBER, Day 218: Naïve Realism

Do you consider yourself a top performer? If yes, then there is almost a 100% chance that you've suffered from "naïve realism" at some point during your life. In his book *Chatter*, Ethan Kross explains naïve realism is a cognitive bias in which you believe with 100% certainty that what you're perceiving is reality, instead of a subjective version of reality seen through your eyes only.[3]

As a top performer, you likely have millions of past experiences in which you successfully matched your reality with a behavior that generated a reward and/or received praise. You did X and achieved Y. You sent an email template and booked a demo. You took a certain route and got to your destination. You shared an opinion and someone agreed. These past experiences and successes are extremely helpful in building confidence and more often than not, lead to more rewards and praise in the future.

Over time, however, we start to become naïve about our version of reality, and we get tricked into thinking, "My perception of reality is 100% accurate because I always get the reward." As you can imagine, this becomes problematic when we disagree with the beliefs, ideas, and/or perspectives of another person. When we fall victim to naïve realism and fail to consider that other versions of reality exist and cannot accept that every person is thinking, feeling, and seeing something different, we stop listening. We stop being compassionate, curious, and we stop trying to understand.

This can lead to destructive situations in which leaders become frustrated and try to impose their versions of reality on others using their authority. For example, when a top performer in a leadership position perceives a struggling sales rep as "lazy" and puts them on a PIP versus considering a different version of reality where the rep is underperforming because they are feeling scared or burnt out.

So today, if you're feeling frustrated with another person on your team, pause and ask yourself: What could be wrong about what I'm perceiving? What might that other person be perceiving? What question can I ask to learn more about their reality?

DECEMBER, Day 219: Stress-Enhancing Mindset

Developing a stress-enhancing mindset can be a quick and easy way to start learning how to use stress to your advantage. According to Dr. Alia Crum, a professor of psychology at Stanford University, this is a mindset in which we perceive stress as something that enhances performance versus something that debilitates performance.

When we adopt this type of mindset, it allows us to seek discomfort and make choices that fuel personal growth within experiences that others are too afraid or too uncomfortable to approach. From Dr. Crum's research, there are three basic steps involved in cultivating a stress-enhancing mindset[4]:

Step 1: Label It

Feeling stressed is uncomfortable, and many of us are not used to embracing this feeling.

Throughout our life, we've been conditioned by millions of articles, videos, and data points that engrained a negative belief about stress in our minds. As a result, we've spent most of our lives acting on behaviors that numb, avoid, and deny what stress feels like. In doing so, we've spent too much time in our comfort zone, otherwise known as the low-stress and low-growth zone. It's only when we can label stress—see it and feel it—that we can learn to work with it rather than against it.

Step 2: Find the Positive in It

Dr. Crumb says we only stress about the things we care about. We're working on a meaningful project, disagreeing with someone we care about, or we're having trouble communicating our values and emotions to a manager at work. Growth requires growing pains, and within these uncomfortable moments there is something positive. Lean in, get curious, and embrace what your mind and body are trying to tell you. It's within special moments like these where you find personal fulfillment and enhance your life experience.

Step 3: Use the "Stress Response" to Your Advantage

In response to a stressor (e.g. big project, argument), your body creates an uncomfortable stress response, and Dr. Crumb explains that when we label this discomfort as "bad" or "negative," stress becomes debilitating. But at the right levels and for short periods of time, these adaptations are extremely positive. Like a superhero with powerful abilities, these helpful changes allow us to focus for longer, make us stronger, process information faster, and retain new knowledge better. The discomfort you feel initially is temporary, and like an engine struggling to start on a cold day, your brain needs time to heat up.

Next time you start to feel stressed today, come back to this page and use these three steps to enhance your growth. Remember, feeling stressed can be a good thing at the right dose.

DECEMBER, Day 220: Sleep Best Practices

I'm fortunate enough to be one of those people who regularly achieves 100% of my sleep needs almost every night. But it wasn't always the case, and when I first started working in sales I suffered from extreme bouts of insomnia and inconsistent sleep. Below are a few of the less conventional things I do to maximize my sleep:

1. **My girlfriend and I sleep in separate bedrooms.**

    We've been together for seven and a half years and couldn't be happier. I truly believe separate bedrooms have played a huge factor in better sleep and a healthier relationship. When we're both rested and have slept well, we can be better partners for each other.

2. **Brown noise running all night.**

    I'm not sure where the popularity of white noise came from, but brown noise has a much lower frequency and is more conducive to sleep. It will sound more like the drum of an airplane versus a static TV. If you search "brown noise" on Spotify you should be able to find a 90 minute track that you can play on repeat all night.

3. **Try to eat nothing after 7 p.m.**

    I'm a big believer of the benefits of intermittent fasting, and my feeding window is from 11 a.m. to 7 p.m. each night. Not only does this take the pressure off my digestive system, but it means I'm not woken up by major digestion issues in the middle of the night.

4. **Wear a sleep tracker, even if seeing data on sleep makes you nervous.**

    According to the American Academy of Family Physicians, people who define themselves as poor sleepers could be suffering from "paradoxical insomnia".[5] This happens when we misperceive how well we sleep or report severe insomnia without objective evidence of sleep disturbances or significant impairments of daytime functioning. Though never formally diagnosed with paradoxical insomnia, I would consistently wake up each morning thinking I under-slept. Wearing a WHOOP provided me with objective sleep data to counter these beliefs and showed I was in fact getting healthy levels of sleep each night. In turn I felt more confident in my ability to sleep, which led to less anxiety when trying to fall asleep.

These strategies may not work or be available to everyone, but hopefully at least one will help move the needle on how well you're sleeping each night.

DECEMBER Endnotes

1. Holiday, R., and Hanselman, S. (2017). *The Daily Stoic Journal: 366 Days of Writing and Reflection on the Art of Living*. Profile Books.
2. Baumeister, R. F., Bratslavsky, E., Finkenauer, C., and Vohs, K. D. (2001). "Bad is stronger than good." *Review of General Psychology*, 5: 323–370.
3. Kross, E. (2022). *Chatter: The Voice in Our Head and How to Harness It*. Vermilion.
4. "Dr. Alia Crum: Science of Mindsets for Health and Performance." *The Huberman Lab* podcast #56. January 24, 2022. https://youtu.be/dFR_wFN23ZY.
5. "Paradoxical Insomnia: Misperception of Sleep Can Be a Tormenting Experience." *Am Fam Physician*. 2017, 95(12): 770. https://www.aafp.org/pubs/afp/issues/2017/0615/p770.html.

AFTERWORD: Salience Bias

SALIENCE BIAS REFERS to the fact that individuals are more likely to focus on items or information in their environment that are more prominent to them and ignore those that feel less important.

There are nationwide mental health days, Mental Health Awareness weeks or months, and workshops that are great at creating a lot of temporary salience around talking about mental health in the workplace. You have now reached the end of this book, and the information and actions you have taken have likely created a lot of salience around mental health in sales. If you read through these pages on your own, do you now focus and think about improving your mental health more? Have these thoughts become more salient? If you read through this book with your team, stop for a moment and look around. Are people talking about mental health more? Has mental health become more salient in your culture?

Start thinking about how you can keep making mental health more salient and visible on a day-to-day basis. Up until now, most of us have all worked in sales environments that reinforced we should fear talking about our mental health. We all have some degree of salience bias that wants us to revert to old habits. Keep having discussions and keep practicing. Together we can reverse the fear of talking about mental health within sales and amplify the march toward peak sales performance.

About the Author

WITH OVER A decade of sales experience, Jeff understands the importance of mental health in achieving peak sales performance.

Battling anxiety, insomnia, and panic attacks early in his sales career, Jeff was forced to confront his struggles with mental health head-on. In doing so, he learned practical research-based strategies that any seller or sales leader could use to manage stress and prevent burnout in sales.

When he was diagnosed with testicular cancer in 2018, his purpose to help sales teams became even more clear when his deep understanding of mental health and strategies involving mindset, resilience, and stress management, which made him successful in sales, also aided in his swift recovery.

Jeff is now the founder of the Sales Health Alliance, which is a company dedicated to creating more awareness around mental health in sales and helping sales teams optimize performance through better mental health.

Index